"Child, What In The Hell Is Wrong With You?"

To mother Margaret, God bless you for your life and sacrifice.

Rev Rudy 5/22/08

By Rev Rudolph Stewart III
"Rev Rudy"

ISBN 0-9741526-0-9

Published by Mtume & Associates, Washington, DC

For ordering books, to schedule book signings, preaching engagements, or workshops/lectures visit Pastor Rudolph Stewart III at www. sankofachurch.org.

Rev. Rudolph Stewart III
P.O. Box 41335, NE
Washington, DC 20018
202-396-7422
www.sankofachurch.org

Dedication

This book is dedicated to my intelligent and beautiful wife Jerlys Diane Stewart. You are my inspiration to write this book. Your work and commitment as a reading coordinator and educator of African American children for over thirteen years, give me hope to keep teaching and preaching for our African nation. All my accomplishments as a man, by God's grace, exist only because of your strength and support. You are to me what day is to night, what sky is to moon and what water is to land. You are my honey and my soft beckoning call of passion from a hostile and bitter world. I love you and without exaggeration could not live my life without you. This work is also dedicated to my three children Imani Diane, Rudolph IV and Jeriah Diane. You all have inspired the title of this book and your love for me reminds me that I am KING and number one in your lives. Your love fortifies me from the abuses I face from society as a man of African descent living in America. Thank you so much. I love you all.

TABLE OF CONTENTS

Acknowledgements

This book is written with grateful acknowledgement to:

My ancestors and elders of the human race who gave their lives fighting injustice and humanity's cruelty to others who have been on the bottom at various points in the history of the world. In addition, they have paved the way and treaded the stony road that I might be able to speak boldly and prophetically.

My grandparents in Wilmington, N.C., Marion Williams and Rudolph Stewart, Sr. My grandmothers Elizabeth Williams and Lily Stewart whose faith has brought me this far and encouragement has lifted me up when life has beaten me down. My granddad Rudolph Senior, taught me through his life, how to press on in the midst of adversity. He had polio ever since he was eight. He had a hump on his back and slept on both knees but I never heard him complain and he always told me to honor God for life. It is because of his example that I am adamant about people calling me by my full name, Rudolph Stewart III. It is not to sound distinguished for I do not seek man's glory, but it is to pay honor to him.

My father, Rudolph Stewart, Jr., and my mother, Norma Jean Stewart, who gave to me from the depths of their souls everything I ever needed even though that meant sacrificing their own goals and dreams so that my life would be one of service to others. Also special love is extended to my sisters, Katrina Stewart, LaShon Adams, Tanya Walker, Yvette Clinton; and to my brothers, Bruce Adams, James Gallmon, Tony Givens, Gerald Luke,

David & Paul Arnett, Ronnell James; my nephews, Kevin Lewis and Reginald Clark; my nieces, Giovanni Clark, Kisha Clark and Breanna Adams; and to my Godchildren: Jasmine Clinton, Sierra Clinton, Malik Jefferson, Omari Jefferson and Malik Shingler.

My Pastor Willie F. Wilson. His teachings and courage as an African man living in America has shaped my understanding of the words "pride, resiliency and Holy boldness." The orator I am today is because of his vision and understanding that leaders in the African American community are born, shaped and groomed in the church.

To the Union Temple Baptist Church Family with special love to Carolyn Beckwith who typed the original manuscript and Toni Stevenson who initially revised the work.

To Rev. Adama Melitte Zawadi who has spent countless hours honing this manuscript, giving divine insight and suggestions in creating a finished product. Also Alinayu Oding for designing the cover.

To Rev. Dr. Cain Hope Felder, internationally renowned biblical scholar, author, preacher, teacher and a beautiful human being. I appreciate your encouragement and persistence in pushing me to deny the myth that African American preachers can either teach or preach but cannot do both. It has been your example and encouragement that awakened the desire for biblical scholarship in my life. Thank you for reaching back and helping me out the pot.

Foreword

Few can deny that the popular culture of The United States of America tends to glamorize and otherwise lay emphasis on youth – being young, feeling young, and looking young, despite one's actual age. It may not be going too far to say that, in America and much of the Western world that our nation has come to influence heavily, most adults are encouraged to bow before the altars of youth. At the same time, the troubling oddity, in all of this, is that many teenagers and young adults are themselves often confused and alienated. They are often without helpful role models that would normally come from persons who are supposed to be – and act like – responsible parents, teachers, public figures and leaders in other respects.

Quite frankly, I do not envy the youth of America Today, especially African American youth. These young people of "the darker hue" face enormous challenges, like never before, as the *de facto* public enemy number one in America. It is distressing indeed that much of the White majority culture so often seems to delight in stereotyping and demonizing Black young people whose efforts at self-development are often willfully undercut virtually at every turn. What is most painful about this tragic domestic reality is that the Black Church should be the one place where a difference for the development of Black youth could really take place.

Sadly, in many instances, the African American Church – despite its rhetoric to the contrary – has come to place little budgetary and programmatic emphasis on these young people whether or not they are part of the immediate church family. In the rural areas, Black youth are either seen as an idle irritant or a delightful appendage some times humored, other times disciplined. In the urban context, if and when Black youth are involved in church activities, they are corralled in the traditional type of Sunday school and/or poorly attended and understaffed Christian teen clubs modeled from mainline denominations. This situation in most of the Black Church with reference to the welfare and prospects of much of her actual and potential youth is more than disturbing; it is frightening! One need only ask any minister in the Black Church, "What percentage of your church's budget is earmarked for work with youth and children?"

One person who has devoted much of his ministry to challenging African American young people with a vigorous Gospel-understanding of life as an empowering alternative to alienation, "gang-banging" and the like is Rev. Rudolph Stewart, III of Washington, D.C. As a young minister, cultivated in the Afro-centric, empowerment Christian ministry of the remarkable Union Temple Baptist Church, "Rev. Rudy" (as he frequently refers to himself) had gained much from years of urban spiritual tutoring by the Reverends Willie and Mary Wilson. Although deeply involved in designing and hosting church-based youth work, as well as radio and cable television Christian outreach programs for Black youth, Rev. Rudy refused to be satisfied with his natural leadership gifts and people skills. In fact, he pursued his undergraduate studies at Howard University as a young man on a mission to reject the "No's" that America so often flings into the faces of numerous African Americans. Few were surprised when he entered the Howard University School of Divinity's three-year Master of Divinity Program, which he finished at the top of his class.

Several of us, as his theological professors, could easily discern that in Rev. Rudy we had no ordinary soul who needed to be behind somebody's pulpit! Here was a fine mind within a keen, disciplined and discerning spirit who had a dynamic unfolding ministry to Black youth that was not going to be silenced or undermined in any way. He has become a frequent invited speaker at youth assemblies in different parts of the country. In fact, one cannot but note with pride the way in which Rev. Rudy and his wife have underscored their commitment to Black youth by quickly developing their own family with two daughters and a son. Both he and his wife, Jerlys, joined us on one of the Study Tours of Egypt and Israel a few years ago, as sponsored by the Biblical Institute for Social Change. Our respective families have all the more bonded in the mutual commitment that we have made to the wit-ness of the church and to the empowerment of the people of God – not the least of those that have sprung from the loins of Mother Africa and the African Diaspora.

Each entry in this provocative book confronts difficult issues with which many a Black youth has to cope today. The author's deft strategy in identi-fying problems and possible solutions is a welcomed contribution to the cor-pus of this kind of literature. Rev. Rudy has served ably as both my Graduate Assistant in New Testament Studies at the Divinity School and more recent-ly as my Teaching Assistant in an undergraduate course at Howard. Consequently, I have come to pay high tribute to his abilities and insights that have effectively and consistently connected him with many a teen and young adult.

With these impressive credentials, academic and hard won in the urban street, Rudolph Stewart III has culled from his collection of sermons and exchanges of a different sort for a wider audience of Black youth, their par-ents and others who seek to work with them in Christian outreach. He has been robbed at gunpoint by Black urban youth; and yet has remained undaunted in trying to reach out with the power of the Gospel to help many of them!

This book is "straight from the heart", but it also makes substantive and deep observations form a mind of candor, tempered by realism and even some humor. This brother, *has been there and done that*; and yet, has not only survived to tell the story, but who cannot but "tell it!" As one reads these reflections, meant to engage our youth and others who have the privi-lege of working with them, one captures glimpses of a truly committed man-child of God who knows whence he has come and what he must never for-get to pass on for the liberation of his people.

Rev. Rudy could easily have written each of the entries that appears in this book from a more elevated, technical and scholarly style. While that

would perhaps have impressed some people, it would have defeated his purpose by making this volume virtually unintelligible and tedious for his tar-
get audience! I am glad that Rev. Rudy is now, with this book, moving to the
next level. I enthusiastically recommend this book to all who minister to
youth in the Black Church or otherwise attempt to work at shaping afresh
and polishing many of them as "diamonds in the rough"! This is a sobering
but, thank God, encouraging and hopeful "*word from the Word*" that refuses
to be made trivial and irrelevant in this time of critical need.

Rev. Cain Hope Felder, Ph.D.
Professor, Howard University School of Divinity and
Chairman, The Biblical Institute for Social Change, Inc.
Washington, D.C.

Introduction

"Child, What in the Hell is Wrong with You?"

This is a question that has lasted throughout many generations of parenting, in particular in the African American community. However, the African American community does not have the copyrights on this question. This cry of perplexity begging for some sort of answer has been and can be superimposed on any community raising children who at some point in there growth and development, do things that causes parents, leaders, preachers, teachers and the like to ask the question, "Child, What in the hell is wrong with you?"

Most of us who follow the teachings of Jesus Christ can verify that hell has always been deemed a curse/bad word. Many have been correctly taught that there are only two types of curse words or phrases in the Bible: To call someone a fool and to curse somebody to hell. As a minister and defender of the gospel of our Lord Jesus Christ, I rest comfortably in the fact that in asking this question I am doing neither. However, I am suggesting that there are times during the course of raising children that parents and various other adults alike have had to ask their child what in the hell or what in the crazy, burning, brainless, desolate area of Hades/ hell was going on in your head when you willing did thus and so?

You may think that Christian parents who love the Lord and worship the Lord in spirit and truth, would be immune to falling to the use of this question, but not so. You would think that after all the choir rehearsals, communions, baptisms, fellowships, usher meetings, visitations of the sick and anniversary celebrations that God would have so polarized Christian parents from falling victim to the lost of patience and the resorting to asking their children this question, but I tell you painfully the answer is still no. In the African American community, parents have seen racism to the highest degree and have felt what it feels like to be public enemy number one. We know first hand the feelings of being taken for granted, used, abused and lied on by the doctors and lawyers and police persons. Tried unjustly. Falsely accused. Having a history of being tortured, lynched, raped, murdered, victimized in the media and erased from American history books. We have had our native land demonized and vilified. I mean throughout all of these horrors and more God has blessed us with a spiritual immunity that allows us to still forgive. God fortified us with the anointing to be able to still work with our oppressors and their heirs. You would think after making it through what we have gone through that raising children would be a piece of cake. You would think there is nothing that a child could humanly do that would force a people so immunized by God's spirit to break down and say out of confusion and frustration, "Child, what in the Hell is wrong with you?"

I am here to bear witness to you that there is no immunity when raising children. I know and remember when growing up how daddy and mama used to say to me "That is okay one day you will grow up and have children of your own and you will get back exactly what you are giving to me." Points of fact all parents have said this at some point to their children. But daddy and mama lied. They forgot to tell us that it would come twice or thrice as hard as we gave it out. They forgot to tell us that at some points in our child's development an alien would inhabit their bodies, as Bill Cosby states so prophetically in his comedy stand up routine, and force them to act and do extra terrestrial type things. They either forgot or purposely elected to not mention the numerous times that we as parents would be sitting, standing, crying or talking on the phone with our children asking them this question, "Child, what in the hell is wrong with you?"

I have witnessed parents losing their last ounce of patience in grocery stores, the malls, shoe stores, restaurants, PTA meetings and yes even church and church activities. I have heard with my own ears, Christian God fearing parents, having been dumbfounded and flabbergasted by the actions of their child ask them this question. Their beautiful gems, blue diamonds and nations that will carry their names on once they depart this world. Their anointed seeds who will promote the advancement of the race. They have said to these children on more than four million occasions, "Child, what in the hell is wrong with you?"

My father and mother on many occasions have had to ask my sisters Trina and Shon after having done something's inexplicable to human consciousness "What in the hell is wrong with yall?" (They's country) I mean if it was not for my good Christian behavior as a child, to balance off the crazy actions of my two aforementioned siblings, My parents would have either gone crazy or would have been locked up for child murder.

What make matters worst in most instances are not necessarily the actions that provoke this question and not even the asking of the question or even the hearing of this question by the child. What is more shocking and mentally arresting is often times the response given by the child in the form of "I don't know." I mean if you could copyright one phrase and get rich off of it would be the child's response of "I don't know." Parents, as painful, confusing and frustrating as it is to hear this response to your question, it is more confusing when you have to accept that in most instances they don't know. Many times our children cannot explain what prompted them to do that or say that or act this way or that way. The brain fails them and words just refuse to line up and come out of the oral cavity in a manner sufficient enough to keep you from going absolutely crazy. But we cannot be all hard on our children. It was the mature, divinely inspired messenger Paul who even found a loss for words when trying to describe his actions as contrary to the will of an all loving God who saved him from a continued life of destruction. He says in the seventh chapter of his letter to the church at Rome, that he has no understanding of what he is doing for the right thing that he really desires to do he does not do, but the thing that he hates he continues to do. I mean surely if the great evangelist Paul found himself in situations where his actions did not line up with his teachings or beliefs, then children who have not yet lived and experienced life to even life's third justifiably should be able to say like Paul and I paraphrase "I don't know what in the hell is wrong with me."

I believe it is because our children live in a world here in America that is constantly confusing them as to who they are, where they come from and what to believe in as intelligible human beings. They live in a media culture of MTV, BET and Hollywood, that suggest in many instances that wrong as you teach in the home is right in the world and the right that you teach in the home is wrong in the world. I mean certainly one can sympathize and empathize that inside their minds they are just as confused about living and life as you are about why they make some of the decisions that they make. The world calls homosexuality, lesbianism and transsexuality, an alternate life style and you call it a sin and perversion against the will of God. What message do you think they hear more, your teachings or the radio, TV, magazine articles, peers, videos and movies? The world says that Columbus discovered America and you teach them correctly that Native Americans were here before Columbus and that they had a civilization more advanced then the one Columbus came from. What message do you think they hear more, yours or the textbooks they read from first grade through college? The world says that there is no racism so you do not have to excel in your studies just focus on being an athlete and you teach true education is the answer not book sense but knowledge of yourself and your history and then the world's history. Again, what message do you think they hear more, the sports celebrity's whose shoes they are wearing or yours in the home?

It is no longer confusing when you really sit back and carefully analyze the contrasting messages being fed to our children on a daily basis. It then is only logical that we find ourselves being forced to break down and ask this question to our children seemingly everyday in most instances or at least weekly if you are lucky.

The comforting message is that we are not by ourselves in resorting to this question in attempting to ascertain an answer to our children's crazy actions. I am sure using my divine imagination that God asked this question when Cain lied about not knowing Abel's whereabouts. I am sure that God after giving Moses instructions to hit the rock one time for water and Moses hit the rock twice, asked this question to Moses. It is for certain that God asked Samson this question after he finally told Delilah where his strength lay knowing that she was going to destroy him. Without any doubt in my mind, God asked this question to Elijah when after God showed up at the battle of Mt Carmel and destroyed the false prophets and Elijah hearing that Jezebel wanted to kill him he left and hid in a cave. And as you will see in the final chapter of this book, it is for certain that Joseph and Mary asked the young Jesus this question after discovering that he left their company on his own, went back to the temple and they having finally located his whereabouts had to ask him, Child. "What in the hell is wrong with you?"(Rev Rudy's version).

This book of biblical lessons/sermons to youth and parents is aimed at divinely answering this question; "Child, What in the hell is wrong with you?" that youth cannot answer in many instances to themselves or to you their parents. There is something missing in the communication between parents and youth. There is something missing in the transmission of moral precepts from parents to youth. There is a void in the spirit of our African American youth. The preacher and teacher have not filled it and in many instances parents are trying to replace it with material things.

When Ezekiel, the prophet, was taken to the valley of dry bones, his vision, as recorded in the 37th chapter of his book, says that he saw bones that were very dry because of a lack of hope. God's message to His people through the prophet, Ezekiel, was a message of hope. He was to deliver this message to our biblical ancestors who, at that point in their history, found themselves in a cultural and social climate that yielded little promise for the future. It is sadly accurate that many youth in the African American community find themselves devoid of hope for the future. Many do not want to hear about the struggles of the past. They are not interested in how far their parents walked to school bare-footed and how college might not have been an option because of poverty. They have no pride in themselves or in their culture. They mirror the bones that are mentioned in Ezekiel's prophecy. God asked Ezekiel the question, "Can these bones live?" a question that Ezekiel rightly knew that he could not answer, but was certain that God could. In resurrecting the spirit of the bones, God commanded Ezekiel to speak and prophesy to the bones. It is my belief that far too many teachers, preachers, parents and relatives have ceased to speak life to our youth. We readily remind them when they mess up or drop the ball, but we forget to have the positive prophecy outweigh the negative. This is why the Black Church has always played a critical role in the lives of the youth in the African American community.

Throughout its history, the Black Church has been responsible for producing the world's foremost orators, scholars, teachers and scientists. A short look backwards at our history in this country would show that in most instances, the only place for an African American to develop and hone God-given talents was in the Black Church in front of its congregation. It should be made clear, however, that ever since the birth of the Black Church, there have always been two different types of Black Church. On the one hand, there was the church that the Euro-American slave owner oversaw and approved of Black folk conducting. Then there was the Free Black Church that was hidden from the sell-out slave preachers and their slave masters.

The former was the church that preached and taught total allegiance to the slave masters and how we should accept our condition as one that God has ordained. This church was the one in which the Black preacher dressed up real nice looking, like a carbon copy of the White preacher. He was instructed by his puppet master to keep the slaves in control by preaching a watered down, Westernized version of the teaching of Christianity. If he could do this faithfully, this preacher was rewarded. This first church never talked about rebellion, revolution or freedom here on earth. It never preached about having earthly possessions as a God-given right for all humanity, not just European humanity. This church only spoke about the "sweet by and by" and "pie in the sky" religion that encouraged slaves not to look for anything here on earth but to gratefully await their reward in heaven. This was not the church that raised leaders and orators. Only a selected few hand-picked by the master were able to speak to the congregation. It was also in this church that the inaccurately, irresponsibly interpreted teachings of the Apostle Paul were preached and drilled into the heads of the first puppet Black preachers and then to the gullible congregants hungry for the Word. These teachings gave gospel validation to the slavery of the Africans in America and used the Africans' belief in Jesus Christ and the Almighty God to try and keep slaves submissive in the Diaspora.

The other Black Church was what E. Franklin Frazier called the "Invisible Institution". It was here that slaves were energized and educated to their purpose as divine beings created in the image of God. In this house were the preachers who spoke about mental liberation. These preachers put their lives on the line by allowing God to show them fresh revelation on the Word of God as well as on their situation as oppressed people living in slavery. The sermons and worship experiences were committed to keeping alive certain Africanisms that survived despite the horrors of the Middle Passage. So, in this church you would witness the ring shout or people "catching the Holy Spirit" and doing the Holy dance. This type of emotional worship was and still is rooted in the various tribal dances of Africa. This was the Black

Church that allowed youth to develop their gifts and become what God had created them to become.

Today many of the singers, orators and leaders of our community trace their roots back to the Black Church. But sadly, in far too many Black Churches across America, the once sharp minds that were cultivated in the church under the supervision of God-fearing adults now often grow dull being pacified, crushed and shackled up in tradition and Christian complacency. Although there are some churches still edifying youth and realizing that the youth are not the future but the present, the majority of the churches seem to have allowed our children to starve to death on empty calories of religious rhetoric and as a consequence they become hopeless.

The final chapter of this work is a message to the traditional Black Church. It is entitled "The Power of Breaking Tradition". It is a message that I pray will break the fetters that threaten to bind the next generation of church leaders. By hiding behind the false veil of tradition, our churches seem to be stifling our young people and forcing them into the hip-hop world. Youth who used to be able to express themselves in church now find it almost sacrilegious to do so in the house of God.

It is my prayer that the Black Church will return to the old landmark of the "Invisible Institution" that birthed and encouraged leaders in our community and gave God the Glory. Because this is a message primarily for the youth, I have intentionally simplified the analysis of select Bible passages. I pray that you enjoy the book and that you heed the messages of hope and liberation for our youth and parents.

For it states in the Book of James 1:23
If you hear a good message and don't obey it, you would be like a man who looks in the mirror and when he walks away he forgets his own face.

This miracle of Jesus casting demons into swine is part of the triple tradition, meaning it finds its story told in three of the four gospels. Its parallels are found in Matt: 28-34 and Luke 8:26-39. This miracle story is told immediately after Jesus calms the Sea of Galilee and just before he heals Jairus' daughter. It seems as though Jesus has just shown His power over nature by calming the seas and now shows His power over the spiritual world by exorcising the demons out of this young man.

The Power in a Name
What is Your Name?
Mark 5:1-9

My grandfather, Rudolph Stewart Senior, taught me through his life how to press on in the midst of adversity. He had polio ever since the age of eight. He always told me to honor God for life. I am adamant about people calling me by my full name, Rudolph Stewart III. It is not to sound distinguished, but it is to pay honor to my grandfather. When my name is called, his legacy lives on in me. I cannot ascertain why people willingly elect to leave off "the third" when pronouncing my name. However, I am not alone in feeling this way. What is of monumental importance to most people is their name. If you really want a good fight, mess up someone's name. The name is so important that you cannot carry on a conversation with a stranger longer than a few minutes without ascertaining that person's name. Young brothers will tell you in a New York minute that a true player or "mack," for older brethren, is keenly aware that first you have to get that sister's name. You were assured a base hit if she gave you her name. Even if you did not have the guts to go up and ask that sister her name, you asked her friend.

Throughout African history, and in particular biblical history, a person's name carried significant spiritual power. There was a time when we would name our children names that held special meaning. In many instances, these names were associated with historical figures that fought for social or religious justice or biblical heroes and heroines of the faith. Even if some folks did not have the name that they liked, as they got older they changed their names. Many found, as they matured, that their names did not fit the purpose God had given them in life.

Once you know a person's name, you know something about their identity. You know something about that person's family. When you really know a person's name, you know how much time the parents prayed and meditated over what they would name their children. There are people we meet today that when you learn their name you may say, "What were your father and mother thinking about when they named you?" We say it jokingly, but we are as genuine as possible without being insulting or mean. I make it a point to ask people, not only "What is your name?" but also "What does your name mean?" You would be surprised at how many people do not know what their name means. It might not seem like a big deal to you right now, but you will see as we go further along in this text that a person's name is a big deal. What has become apparent to me, ministering to youth all across the country, is the painful fact that our young folk are responding to names that were not given to them by the Lord. They are responding to names that have been placed on them by a European supremacist history and present-day society. So many of our ancestors grew up having to respond to the name "nigger," "ape," "coon," "shiftless," "no-good," etc. They had to endure those names, but it was a God-presence down on the inside that made them know that through Jesus their name was synonymous with royalty. They knew and felt that what they were being called by society did not determine who they were. They may have had to walk with their head down, but they walked with an inner pride because they knew they were a royal priesthood and a chosen generation. It does not seem that our young folk today have that same fortitude. Many of our young girls are responding to the name "ho" (whore), "freak," "hood rat," "swamp rat," "chicken head," "doms," "femmes" and "aggressives". They are responding to the name of being sexually active prematurely before really understanding what sex is and the purpose for which God created it. They are responding to names that were not given to them by God. Our young brothers appear to be responding to names that have been placed on them as a badge of honor, but it is really a badge of shame. They are responding to "gangbanger," "dumb jocks," "dogs," "violent animals," and "niggas" just to name a few. They have not been taught that names are spiritual and self-fulfilling. Their lives have been shaped by what people have called them. So many people have been called "bastards" while growing up because many fathers were not in the home. Many walked in that name. Because of low self-esteem, it took the Almighty God to change that name. Young folks are responding to the name "inferior" and "minority" and other negative names.

As we look at the text, Jesus has just finished performing a miracle over nature on the Sea of Galilee. We find that when He came off the boat a young man possessed with demons ran up to Jesus. Matthew's recording states that there were two young men, and it is probably true, but for the sake of consistency I will just record, as Mark did, that only one of them came up to Jesus. The text says that the minute that young man saw Jesus from afar he ran and worshiped him and cried out, "What have I to do with you, Jesus, Son of the Most High God? I implore you by God that you do not torment me." Jesus said to him, "Come out of the man, unclean spirit!" Then He asked him, "What is your name?" The interesting observation I find here is that nowhere else in the biblical record does Jesus ask someone his or her name. When He called Peter, He did not ask Peter what his name was. When He called Nathaniel, He did not ask what his name was. He knew his name. When the woman with the issue of blood touched His garment, He did not turn around and say, "Who touched me and what is your name?" It is only here when Jesus was speaking to someone who had an unclean spirit did He ask what was his name. What is more intriguing is the fact that Jesus had previously healed a young boy by exorcism in the temple and did not ask that demon its name (1:23-26). This time the Lord had to identify who this young person was. This young boy had been called so many names that he did not know who he was. He had no idea. He had no idea the purpose that God had put in him. He had no idea that God had laid out for him something special because society was calling him a man with an unclean spirit. It seems as though society placed on this young man names that shaped his identity. The text says he was possessed, meaning he was evil and out of control. We see this today in present-day society. Society calls many of our youths "possessed". I believe this young man was called "possessed" and "violent" so often that he allowed the spirits associated with these names to enter into him. The story tells us that not only did he lose his identity, but also he moved away from civilization. He no longer lived with the ordinary people. He no longer was in the regular educational system. He was considered hyperactive, so he was now in special education. He was no longer considered clean because he had been called a pimp so much. He put so much emphasis on being a pimp that he contracted HIV/AIDS and now he was no longer a part of civilization. The Bible says that he made his living in the graveyard. He made his living where other folk dead in the spirit made their living. Young people, when you do not know what name to respond to, you will begin attracting and hanging out with "dead" folk. Young brothers in junior high and high school make sure that the name you are walking in does not attract other brothers who want to be pimps, hustlers and gangbangers. Make sure you are not walking in a dead name that says it is okay to be sexually promiscuous; all I have to do is wear a condom. Please do not walk in that name because that name will let you know that when the condom breaks, society will give you another name and that name will be "teen father" and/or "HIV/AIDS positive." They will give you another name. It will be "STD positive" and whenever you receive these names, the same society that gave you these names will be the very same society that will write you off. Young girls do not walk in the name that BET (I call it Buffoon Entertainment Television) has given you. Do not walk in the name that Snoop Dog, Lil' Kim and the Hip-Hop world have given to you. If you walk in that name, you will begin to think that your breasts and your body are what is most important. You will begin to think that that is where your value is and if you walk in that physical name, then all you will attract are boys trying to get your breasts and trying to get your body.

One of the myths or stereotypes used by those Europeans who came to Africa to steal Africans and make them slaves was the notion that African women were animals. Their sex drive was very high and their bodies were built to seduce men into having sex with them. America continues to promote those stereotypes through Hollywood productions, the Hip-Hop world and the like. Dr. Kelly Brown Douglas in her book, Sexuality and the Black Church states that through the stereotype of Black women as sexually insatiable animals, the structure of European supremacy will continue. This means that the dominant power will continue to abuse you and enslave you because they feel you have no mental control over your sexuality and logically all animals need to be tamed and trained. If you act and think like your body is where your divine value is then you dishonor all your mothers, grandmothers and great grandmothers who were raped, murdered and who were forced to participate in sex trains with brutal, sick European men.

If you walk in the name that rhymes with itch, you will walk in other names as well. You will walk in "high school dropout". You will walk in the name of "fornicator," having sex before marriage. Do not walk in the name of "female dog". Do not walk in the name "nigga:" Do not walk in that name. Young people stop responding to names that God did not give you.

As we look further into the text we see that the people in society, in an attempt to contain this crazy young man, shackled him up. That sounds so familiar, does it not? One of the biggest industries in America is the prison industry. So they call you "crack sellers," "gangbangers," and "thugs". They glamorize thug life and jail life through "OZ" on HBO in order to insure that you will be their future inmates. Even now all across America, young men and women are beginning to walk in the name of "future inmates". You see them walking with their pants hanging down. The people in jail cannot wear belts, but the brothers think it is cool. They are walking in a name that is going to lead them to a big penitentiary with a very small room. The Bible says that he made his living among dead folk. He had lost his identity. He did not know who he was and the question that Jesus asked him was aimed at doing three things. The question that Jesus asked this young man, first of all, was aimed at making sure that he could **Identify Who He Was**. You have to identify who you are. Are you Black? Are you a Negro? Are you a Nigga? Are you a pimp, a whore, a stupid athlete? What is your name? What do you respond to? Adults, we must not forget to tell our young folk the different names that we have responded to in our lifetime. Many of us responded to being a teenage mother. I know times were different, but many of us still responded to that name. That tells us not to look down on our young people who might have made a mistake, but to help them lift their head up. Call them a royal priesthood, even though they may have made a mistake. So we cannot forget that that is what Jesus was saying. "What is your name?" He was not talking to the boy. He was talking to the demons inside the boy. It does not matter what your child is responding to presently; even the demons recognize the power of God. They fell down and worshiped Jesus on sight. That is good news for our young folk who might be confused about their real name. Parents, you might be praying for your niece or nephew or for some young folk. You keep calling them righteous names and watch the demons jump up out of them.

The second thing that Jesus' question was aimed at doing was to show the demon and the young man how much **Power is in a name**. The demon's response, "My name is Legion, for we are many," allowed the young man to hear and realize the fact that not only was he unaware of who he was; but that he had so many people inside of him, it is no wonder why he was hanging out among dead folk. His revelation is just like many of our young folks'. "No wonder I am hanging out with people with D averages." Young brothers can now say to themselves, "No wonder I think it is cool to smoke a blunt. No wonder I am crazy. I have let so many demons get inside of me that I do not know what is right anymore." There is power in the name. There have been many people throughout our powerful history who have recognized what this young man had. When Malcolm Little reached this understanding he changed his name to Malcolm X. Many of the conscious revolutionaries began to change their last names because their last names were the slave masters' names. So when they achieved higher levels of consciousness, they said, "I can no longer be called by the slave master's name." So they sanctified themselves by changing their names. You do not have to change your name physically, but you must change your mental and spiritual name.

The Lord showed me that this young man was in the right place at the right time. Jesus shows us, adults, that we should never be afraid to walk in the graveyard. The Bible says that Jesus was walking the graveyard. How many of you know that when Jesus walks down your street, He changes your name? He changes your identity. The elders used to sing, "I told Jesus that it would be all right if He changed my name." When you come into contact with Jesus, you come one way, but you leave differently. This is why in the church there is a saying, "I looked at my hands, they looked new. I looked at my feet, they did too." Just come in contact with Jesus. The Bible says that it is at the name of Jesus that every knee shall bow, every tongue confess that He is Lord. Here is the good news. If the demons bowed down to Jesus, what do you think human beings have to do? If the evil spirits have to recognize who has the power, what do you think world leaders have to do? All you have to know is that this question was aimed to, number one: Identify what his name was. Number two, it was aimed to show this man that there was power in his name. Thirdly, this question that Jesus posed was to show this young man at the end of this story that when you come into contact with Jesus, Jesus will **Change Your Name**. It says in the text that when this young man identified himself as Legion, as being many demons, that Jesus did not get mad. Jesus did not begin to curse. All the text says is that Jesus said to the demons, "Come up out of him."

There were about 2,000 demons in him and not one demon stayed. That is power! Jesus did not have to say, "In my name come out of him," because He is Christ the "anointed one," the "blessed one," and the one with all power. So, when Jesus looked at the demons all he said was, "Flee!" That is what demons do. When you come into contact with Jesus, all you need to know – I do not care what they call you. I do not care what they say about you – when you come into contact with the Lord, He will change your name. When Jesus died, Peter, James, John and Paul began healing people in His name. That is what I like about the song, *Bless that wonderful name of Jesus, salvation in the name, healing in the name of Jesus. Bless His name, no other name I know.*

Finally, 5:18-19 informs us that this young man, after being released from demonic imprisonment, begged Jesus to be with him and Jesus denied this young man. Yes, it does seem strange that Jesus would deny this request. But we must look deeper at this denial. Jesus informs this young man to go back and tell all the people the great things that the Lord had done for him. He had been ex-communicated and talked about but now he was a new creature. He was commissioned by the Lord to become a minister to his own people. He was told to go and cry out loud and let his new voice be heard. He was to tell that the Lord had worked a miracle in his life.

Here then is the final lesson. Young people, regardless of how your teenage life started off; once the Lord releases you from the shackles of sin; once God's mercy expels your demons of laziness, ingratitude, selfishness, perverted, sexual thinking and activity, your marching orders are to go back and tell all your friends, family and school mates what great things the Lord has done for you. Now you become the prophet and evangelist. Now you become the minister and orator. Your past has passed and now, behold, you are become the name "A Royal Priesthood" and a "Chosen Generation".

What is Your Name? Review Questions

1. What are the other Gospels that tell the story of the Gadarene Demoniac? Cite chapter and verses.
2. Cite one difference in the way this story is told that is distinct from the Gospel of Mark.
3. The author teaches that once you know a person's name, you know what about that person?
4. What is unique about the question Jesus asked the young man in the story?
5. List the three reasons why Jesus asked this young man what was his name.
6. Make a list of the positive names people have called you.
7. Make a list of the negative names that people have called you.
8. Name two of your African American ancestors who changed their birth names.
9. Why did they change their names?
10. Using the resource list provided, research the meaning of your name. Then use the resource guide to find an African name that fits your personality.

Resources:

1. Search engine: www.bigmomma.com
2. Asante, Molefi Kete. The Book of African Names;Trenton, N.J.: Africa World Press, 1991.
3. Douglas, Kelly Brown. Sexuality and the Black Church: a Womanist Perspective. Maryknoll, N.Y.: Orbis Books, 1999.
4. Throckmorton, Jr., Burton H. ed. Gospel Parallels: A Comparison of the Synoptic. Gospels: with Alternative Readings from the Manuscripts and Noncanonical Parallels: Nashville: T. Nelson, 1992.
5. Woodson, Carter G. The Mis-education of the Negro. Philadelphia, PA: Hakim's Publications.

This infamous passage of Scripture in Ezekiel is probably one of the most recognizable events in biblical antiquity. It is part of a series of visions and revelations received before the news of the destruction of Jerusalem. It was a message of hope to ease the gloom of the people.

Bony Children from Nazareth
Ezekiel 37:1-6 cf. John 1:46-47

Ezekiel 37:1 records that "the hand of the Lord was upon me and carried me out in the spirit of the Lord and set me down in the midst of a valley which were full of bones." If I can be biblically and theologically bold enough, I want to suggest to you that this valley where God carried Ezekiel was Nazareth.

Nazareth is north of Jerusalem. It is a valley surrounded by tall hedges making it impossible to see into Nazareth. From Nazareth you have to climb up to the edge in order to see the place where Gideon and Barak fought their famous battles. You can see the place where Elijah fought the prophets up on Mt. Carmel. When you climb up out of the valley of Nazareth, you can see the rest of the world.

The public's perception of Nazareth was that it was a bad place. Mind you, the only information outsiders knew about Nazareth was what people said about Nazareth. This is proven by Nathanael's question to Philip in John 1:46, "Can any good thing come out of Nazareth?"

There are two questions that will be the foundation for our discussion. In Ezekiel 37:3, God asked Ezekiel, "Can these bones live?" In John 1:46 Nathanael asked Philip, "Can any good come out of Nazareth?" These two questions seem to be filled with irony. God, the omniscient Creator of heaven and earth is asking one of His creations about the possibility of recreation and resurrection and Nathanael is questioning a mere human creation about the good of Jesus Christ, God incarnate in man. The first question was prophetic and spoke to the future. Nathanael's question dealt with the past. God's question dealt with divine knowledge. Nathanael's question dealt with public perception. God's question was addressed to the spirit of man. Nathanael's question only dealt with man's human limitations.

For the answer to Nathanael's question, let us go backwards in biblical history and look at Ezekiel: 37 where Ezekiel says that the Lord caused him to pass back and forth in the midst of this valley of dry bones. The first divine observation that sheds light on a potential answer is to notice that in passing back and forth, Ezekiel had to **Survey** the bones that were in his midst. If you will, Ezekiel became a spiritual homicide detective. When someone has been murdered or has died, the homicide detective goes to the scene of the crime, puts on his gloves and examines all the evidence that could have contributed to the death of the person. I do not know if you have noticed it, but our African American children are dying. They are starving to death. They are starving because we as parents, teachers, preachers, and mentors have not fattened them up with a relevant Word of God. They are starving because we have not given them a place in this society. They are bony and on the verge of expiring.

There are several conditions that can cause people to become bony. I would like to analyze three. The first condition is *anorexia*. This is a condition in which young people do not see themselves as God created them. They see themselves like Nathanael saw Nazareth, strictly through the public's perception. African American young girls see the mindless animalistic videos and character portrayals that continue to perpetrate the false sexual stereotypes used by European slave masters to justify the need for Africans to be enslaved. They see thin, shapely, carved up women and because the way they see themselves is so different from the way they see themselves portrayed in the media they refuse to eat. The same way they refuse to eat the physical food for life, they refuse the spiritual word of God given them by their parents and the preachers. It does not matter how much you tell them that they are special. It does not matter how much you tell them that there is something sacred about their body. It does not matter that you tell them, "Pull your pants up, son. You are a respectable person." It does not matter that you tell them that they have a future in this God-given land, called America. They refuse to eat what you feed them because their perception of self is shaped by BET, shaped by Snoop Dog, shaped by Bone, Thugs and Harmony, by Lil' Kim Janet Jackson and Missy Elliott to name a few. So they starve themselves to death. They do not eat what you try to feed them.

The second condition is **Bulimia**. This is a condition where even though the same mentality to respond to this American standard of beauty pervades their spirit; the urge to eat overwhelms them. So they go and consume all that they can, but they regurgitate it as soon as they consume it. When it goes inside, it does not find something to attach to so it comes right back up. That sounds like our young people today. They will take in a scripture, a song or a sermon on Sunday morning, but on Monday when their brothers are smoking blunts they regurgitate because their perception is that it is not cool not to smoke.

Young girls will go out and give themselves to anybody. They innocently and mistakenly engage in oral sex and anal sex because they have been duped into thinking that they can still be considered virgins as long as there is no vaginal penetration. Their perception is not to save themselves until they are divinely, economically and socially responsible to begin a family. So they spit back out the words of the preacher in Bible study. Then they end up starving to death, becoming bones right before our eyes. Then we ask the question, "Can these bones live?" Can any good thing come out of the African American ghettos and suburbs of America?

The third condition is a condition we, as adults, pass on to our children. This is not an outside condition. This is a disease that is passed on through the blood stream. You can call it **Sickle Cell Anemia**. It is passed from parent to child. This is why the elders used to say, "the apple does not fall far from the tree." The way our young people are acting and why they are starving to death is because of a condition that we have passed in the blood. Then we pass this condition on in the spirit. This condition says that you can only go so far in the world because of racism. We pass on fear genetically. You were too scared to step out and try something and likewise the young people decide that they are too scared and they stay right in Nazareth. This valley is cut off from the world. This valley of high school dropouts is blocked from high school graduates and college graduates. This valley is where HIV/AIDS is on the increase especially among girls and young women ages 13-24. This valley in Nazareth is where millions of African American men and boys are in jail physically, psychologically, socially and economically. In many instances, we have passed this condition to our children through the blood. The Lord sees our children starving and is saying first of all, survey which condition is killing your children. Survey, parents, what your child knows. A lot of our children are cut off from their history, so when you try to tell them how it was when you were growing up they regurgitate it because there is no sense of African connection within them. You try to tell them of the struggles of how you had to fight for voting rights and they do not want to hear it. You try to tell them about the struggles of Dr. King and tell them about the sojourns of the African slave trade and they do not want to hear it. Anorexic, they do not take it in. They starve because you have not surveyed the fact that the school system just is not going to tell them what they need to know. The educational system here in America is designed to erase everything of African origination and contributions to the world, and in particular, to America. The textbooks are just not going to tell them. Most churches in America are not going to tell them about their African history, sadly, not even the Black church. So, Survey what is going on.

Then God told Ezekiel to prophesy to the bones. **Speak** to the bones. Ezekiel was to speak a message of hope in the midst of despair. What are we saying to our young people? Are you calling them "Generation X"? If you call them "Generation X," then you may eXpose them to a mentality that is not of God. When you call them "Generation X," you may eXpel them out of the church's worship. When you call them "Generation X," you may eXcommunicate them from the knowledge of God's love and will for their lives. When you call them "Generation X," they may eXorcise the Word of God within them and eXpire and become dry bones. The Bible says that death and life are in the power of the tongue. I know you love your child, but what do you say about your child? What do you speak to your child? Do you prophesy to your child and say, "You are more than what you are showing me?" Do you speak to your child and say, "I know you have an F but you can get a C, then you can get a B and then an A? What are you speaking to your child? What are you saying to the dry bones in your homes, in your communities, in your churches? When I was growing up, Granddaddy and Grandmama used to come in and speak to the children while they were asleep. They would come in with the olive oil, lay hands on the child while the child was dead to the conscious world. They would speak to the God in the child and say, "You are a leader. You can make it. I know you can do it. You are God's child. You are better than what the world says. You are the best." You know what that did? That woke up the God in that child. Look at what happens when you speak to those dry bones. When your child goes to school and when they are being pulled by the devil, they do not know why they make the right decision but you know it is the Word of God. They do not know why they went to school instead of cutting class, but you know it was because you laid hands on them. This is why the songwriter wrote Somebody prayed for me, had me on their mind and took the time to pray for me. What are we speaking to our young people? Are we telling them that they are not going to be anything because their daddy was not anything? Are you thinking that you do not want them to be like him? What are we speaking to our children? What are we saying to them? Are we telling them to go on and get their degrees, their Masters degrees and their Ph.Ds; but do not forget where you come from because when you get your degree you have to go back to your community and help somebody else get theirs? Are you telling them that this American dream says, get what you can get and forget about who was pushing and helping you on the way up?

Although Nathanael is asking if any good can come from Nazareth, I have to deal with Ezekiel's response to God and Philip's response to Nathanael because Verse five in Ezekiel says, "The Lord says, 'behold, I will breathe back in you the breath of life so that you can live. I will lay skin and flesh upon these bones and I will cover them up.'" Watch and allow God to show you that God is God. He tells Ezekiel, "I will do it so they Shall know that I am God". Now keep that in your mind because when God asked Ezekiel, "Could these bones live?" Ezekiel said to God, "Only You know." When Nathanael asked Philip, "Can any good come out of Nazareth?" Philip said the one thing we need to tell our children, and ourselves, "Come and See." The Lord says when you survey what is going on; when you begin to speak life to your child; do not worry about the fact that they are living in Nazareth. Do not worry about the fact that they are living in the crack and the blunt houses, and the sex house and the educational mediocrity house. Do not worry about the fact that they are failing in school. Do not worry about the fact that teenage pregnancy is on the rise. Do not worry about the fact that they are dropping out and failing school. You just speak the Word of God. This is what the Lord said. " I am going to do it. Do not worry about it. You do what I say and I am going to raise them up. I am going to resurrect them." Nathanael, you want an answer to your question? Come on in the Book of Ezekiel. The Lord says, "I am going to resurrect these bones just so you Shall know that I am God." Some of you all do not believe in God. You do not believe God can do it. You have lost your faith in God, but I serve a risen Savior. Come and see, Nathanael. Nathanael jumped back in the Book of Ezekiel and all those bones that have been trampled on, all those youth whom we have forgotten, all those youth at the bottom of the economic and educational barrel, we call them the foot bone and the foot bone has been connected to the leg bone; the leg bone has been connected to the thigh bone; the thigh bone has been connected to the hip bone; the hip bone has been connected to the back bone; the back bone has been connected to the head. And guess what some of you found, and others will find out? God is still God. Some of you found out that God is still in the blessing business. How do you know, preacher? I was out there. I sold drugs. I was failing and my mother spoke to the bones. She said, "I caused God to come into your life, not so you could get the glory, but so you will know that God is God. You want an answer to your question? Speak the word of God. Let God be God." He can do it. I used to see people, when I was growing up, and they would say, "That boy ain't going to be nothing. That boy is not going to be anything growing up in Southeast Anacostia Washington, DC. I do not know why his mama is wasting her time." But you know what I say to them? Back then I did not really know who I was or who God was. I did not know what God could do, but look at me now preaching, writing and teaching the Word of God. Can these bones live? Yes. Let God be God!

Bony Children: Review Questions

1. Where is the town of Nazareth located?
2. What are the two questions referenced as the foundation of the chapter?
3. Who asked these questions?
4. Where were they located?
5. Compare and/or contrast these two questions.
6. List the three medical conditions cited that cause people to become bony.
7. Describe these conditions.
8. What three actions did Ezekiel do to make the bones live again?
9. How does the author describe B.E.T.?

This first chapter of Exodus opens with an explanation of the population growth of the Israelites after coming with Jacob to Egypt under the good privilege of Joseph. Verses 1-7 give a genealogy while the focal verses 7-12 speak about the Anatomy of Oppression and an emergency plan of action issued by a new Pharaoh. Scholars agree that this is an outside Hyksos ruler who forced his way into power. This explains why Pharaoh did not know Joseph and why he feared a population explosion.

Public Enemy Number One
Exodus 1:7-12

The fertilization process of human beings is quite fascinating. Young brothers and sisters learn of this process at some point during their junior high school or high school years of academia. It is not difficult to understand. Let us observe a few details about the process that will hopefully set the tone for the upcoming message of prophecy to African American males.

Scientists inform us that a male, upon reaching orgasm, ejaculates some 200,000,000 to 600,000,000 sperm into the vagina of a female. It is worthy to note that it is the male's sperm that is responsible, by the will of God, for determining the sex of the child, whether it will be a boy or a girl. The woman already has an X chromosome. If a male produces an X chromosome that fertilizes the egg, then the baby is a girl. If he produces a Y chromosome, then the baby is a boy. I want you to understand that these 600,000,000 sperm are released at the same time. Out of the 600,000,000 sperm 200,000,000 will make it to their destination. Four hundred million sperm will die because of the acidic environment of the vagina. The acid in the vaginal walls crushes them and they do not make it. One hundred and ninety nine million, nine hundred ninety nine thousand, nine hundred and ninety nine will survive the first attack but will later die. Some of them get detoured. So instead of hitting their destination, they flog off in other places. Some of them get caught up with each other and end up going back and forth. Two hundred million will make it through the environment, 199,999,999 will make it to the destination but only one will achieve its goal. Five hundred and ninety nine million, nine hundred and ninety nine thousand, nine hundred and ninety nine possibilities are destroyed. This fertilization process seems to parallel the process of life among many African American males. So many start off with a clear divine destination but the hostile racist environment crushes them before they reach their goal. Their peers get them playing games all day and they eventually become side tracked. Just as the acid of a woman's vagina kills some 400,000,000 sperm, the acidic environment of American ghettos and suburbs seem to annihilate our young African American males.

What is it about African American boys that appear to make them Public Enemy Number One?

I wondered out loud to God, why are there more girls in college and more boys in jail? Why are there more boys infected with HIV/AIDS, even though the number of girls is growing especially in Washington, DC where the latest statistics show a 33% increase among African American and Latino girls and young women 13-24? Why are there more boys in special education than there are girls? God obviously has anointed the male child for special divine purposes in His creation and celebration of humankind has He not? I mean when you look at the odds of a child becoming a boy, you have to deduce a special calling on a male's life. The Holy record seems to bear witness to this statement. Adam was the first human created by God. Noah was chosen by God to replenish the destroyed earth. Abraham was called to be the father of many nations. Jacob was the father of the 12 tribes. Joseph was ordained to help his family survive. Moses was chosen to liberate his people. All of the Major and Minor Prophets were males. He who would proclaim the coming of our Lord and Savior Jesus Christ was a male. John the Baptist was his name. Jesus Christ the Savior was the Son of God. There were 12 disciples. Although there were women disciples, God chose 12 male disciples. The great Apostle Paul was a male. Indeed, the Holy record seems to bear a consistent witness to the fact that there is something obviously in God's plan for males. (This is not to ignore God's purpose for females, but this is a tailor-made message for males). However, if 400, give or take a few, get side tracked, if 199 reach their destination but fail to achieve their goal, then it seems as though Pharaoh's plan to annihilate pubic enemy number one begins to succeed.

Let us look at the text and try to uncover this plan in biblical times to crush those males, dark-skinned, with woolly hair. The reason was to possibly prevent a liberator from raising the people out of oppression. First of all, after observing the growth of the Hebrews and fearing a day when the Egyptians would physically become the minority Pharaoh said, "Let us deal with them wisely." Are you fully aware that HIV/AIDS has reached epidemic proportions in the African American community? However, the schools are not talking about it. Although the majority population dying from HIV/AIDS is African American, the advertisements and the public service announcements seem to always show other ethnic groups as the victims. This is a design to deal with them wisely. Educational propaganda is dealing with the problem by promoting condom usage as safe sex as opposed to abstinence and spiritual discipline. They just leave it in the air. Unfortunately, where the Black Church used to be the lighthouse of knowledge, many of them are now mausoleums. They do not touch the topic of sexuality, while our children are dying right in front of the preacher. Let us deal with them wisely. Let us keep them ignorant about sex so that when they hit puberty and they begin to smell themselves, young girls will begin to give their bodies away because they do not have any idea about HIV/AIDS. Even though the young males are saved, even though they are in the church, and even though they go through rites of passage ceremonies, when the girls give them the chance outside of Bible study, and outside of Sunday school and when the opportunities present themselves even saved young men would go ahead and sleep with the young ladies. Let us deal with them wisely. Let us tell them that marijuana is from the earth. Let us put it in their community. Let us glorify the media stories that show athletes who smoke marijuana. These happen to be the same athletes, in many cases, whose tennis shoes your children are wearing to school every day. Let us not tell them that there are more chemicals in marijuana than there are in cigarettes. Let us let them kill their brain cells. Let us deal with them wisely. Let us glamorize thug life. Let us let them think that the only way out of the environment to reach their destination is to be a Hip Hop star. Wisely, let us let them know that if they play real hard and spend all their time on the basketball court and football field they, too, could become the next Kobe, Shaq, McNabb, McNair, or Jordan. Let us deal with them wisely, even though only 200 out of a million children ever make it to the NBA or NFL. The text says that Pharaoh set taskmasters over the Hebrews. You can call these taskmasters the American educational system that crafts curriculum to include study materials and books in which nobody you read about looks like you. See Johnny run. See Johnny talk. See Johnny walk, but Johnny does not look like you. In this distorted educational system they teach you about European history. They teach you about Columbus, but they do not teach you about Imhotep, the African mathematician and scientist. They do not teach you about Shaka Zulu. They do not teach you about the great African men and women who fought in the struggle, but let us deal with them wisely. Let us put the educational taskmaster over them so even if we get some that are smart, we will take them away. Give them full scholarships to Yale and other white, stoic schools and we will corrupt their minds so that they are no good to the African American community. When they get their degrees, they will forget to come back home to their community because they are not African American any longer. Let us put taskmasters of religion over them. Let us give them an Italian/Euro Jesus with blond hair and blue eyes, even though the Bible says that He had thick hair, long hair, probably dreadlocks. Let us not give them the Jesus who was a man of color, who was bold enough to turn over tables in the temple when the moneychangers disrespected his Father's house. Let us not give them the Jesus who affirmed who he was.

Pharaoh appointed task masters over them. Let us let the media shape their intelligence. There are no young boys on TV who have power or who are successful. There are no young African American children that you can point to on TV, in the magazines, in the movies who have positive roles. Who are they? Where are they? Point them out to me. Name them. Guess what? Our children watch more TV than other ethnic group. Who are they watching? Let us deal with them wisely because we know that it does not matter what you read, but what you see. Every time you see something, your mind takes a picture. Even though you are striving to be your African self, all you see are buffoons on TV. If all you see are thug life rap puppets on TV, movies stars and athletes, if that is all you see, then that becomes your reality. You begin to say this is all that I can be, so let me not worry about getting an A or B in geometry. Let me just focus on learning how to rap and being a clown in class. Let us put taskmasters over them to force them to build cities for America/Bush, I mean Egypt/Pharaoh. Cities...let us force them to build a city of Tommy Hilfiger, FUBU, Jordan and DKNY. Let us force them to build cities for Korean carryouts. Let us build the city of jails. Let them build a city of Nike, so that even their self-esteem is placed in their shoes. They will not have a problem with shooting and killing for a pair of Nikes because they want to build systems. Let us deal with them wisely. Let us kill the boys and let the girls live. Have you ever taken notice of the fact that nobody is talking about our boys anymore? When was the last time you heard about a murder of a young African American boy on TV? It is still happening, but the media is not reporting it anymore because they want to kill the boys and let the girls live. Women do not threaten the system of white privilege. Men threaten the system. Liberation is not going to come just by a woman. It takes a man; but if they can kill you early – nine, ten, 11, or 12 they do not have to worry about you any more.

Many of our children work their five or six weeks doing summer jobs as well as after school jobs and all they want to do is buy a pair of shoes. Parents work hard to put food in the house and all you want to do is take your three or four dollars to go get chicken wings with mumbo sauce from a Korean. You give your money to someone who does not look like you, to someone who is too scared to live near you. When they close their carry-outs, the Korean owners get in their nice cars and drive out to deep suburbia far away from you animals in the ghetto who do not care about your body or your community. Fish and chicken set on the counter all day long. When you come in the Korean store cooks take it and re-dip it in old grease, but you say, "I love me some chicken wings with mumbo sauce. I can care less how they cook it." You have a greater charge to remember that you are wanted. When they show America's most wanted, they do not show the brothers on there because they want to talk to them, counsel them or rehab them. They want to know if you have seen them and reported them, so they can kill them. I am trying to educate your consciousness so you are working with a new mind. You cannot put on the mind of Christ Jesus and still be the same idiot you were before you were saved. You cannot walk out and say I have a new name, I am Zulu and yet you are the same ignorant person when they pass the dipper you are smoking. Your job is to be educated and then go and educate. Now that you are at this level in your life, you have to walk worthy of the vocation of being called an African man.

As always, there is good news in the text. The Bible says that the more they oppressed the Hebrew boys, the more they multiplied. Let me modernize it. There are systems of European supremacy and African inferiority in place to kill you. There are taskmasters in place to make sure you never know who you are; that you never walk with your head up, that you never look in the mirror and see God, that you never look in the mirror and see Jesus, that you will not apply to the Black schools, that you will never help your brother or sister out and that you will not challenge your brother.

The more they locked you up, flooded your system with STDs and HIV, told you to wear condoms even though condoms fail and told you to father children and not take care of them, even though all these systems are in place, the Lord allows you to continue to multiply. The Lord allows you to continue to reproduce because you are the salvation of your people. If no other king men, soldiers/warriors do it you, reading this book, have to do it. Never forget Pharaoh wants you dead, not…or alive, just dead. He does not mind killing you, but he will not kill you physically because he still needs you to continue to build up his system. If he kills you physically, you cannot buy any more NIKES for $200 when they only cost two or three dollars to make. And that is done by exploiting other children in Third World countries when, instead of consuming, you should be producing. So he does not want to kill you physically, he wants to kill you mentally. He wants to kill your spirit. He wants to kill you so you do not pray to God, even though you come to church. He wants to kill you so when you call on Jesus' name, you cannot turn down that drug or sex when you are in school. He wants to kill you in your education because you think that it is all right to get D's when your counterparts are getting A's and B's. You see Pharaoh does not want to kill you physically because he needs some niggers. Always needs some niggers. Niggers are a hot commodity in America. Slavery has taken a serious toll on African Americans. European slave masters worked hard to ensure that even after slavery would end that psychologically African Americans would still serve the cause of the European supremacists. The people who have never de-programmed themselves to be free from psychological slavery I call "niggers". America continues to flourish economically because niggers do not mind being locked up for 20-30 years in the prime of their lives, working for free, building computers for free while European prison owners sell them to make a nice profit. Niggers do not mind continuing to have sex with men and women and catching HIV/AIDS or herpes while needing medication for the rest of their lives, again making some European who produces the medicine rich. There is always a need for niggers who are going to do whatever the people ask them to do for money and ask no questions. When you look in magazines, you can get killed mentally because you will not see yourself. You will see Tupac, Biggie Smalls and all those other people who sold their souls to be rich. You see the nouveau riche niggers who are slaves but think they are free because they are rich. Pharaoh does not want you dead physically; he wants you dead mentally. So while it is okay for you to speak English and jive, your counterparts are speaking two, three and four different languages at your age. If you do not see anything wrong with it, there is no problem. He will kill you spiritually and mentally so that when you see the Latino population growing and working the jobs your fathers and mothers used to work, and still need to work, it does not bother you. Why does it not bother you? You are not getting straight A's. Who do you think is going to take over the businesses? Who do you think is getting more of the higher paying salaries in corporate America? Who is going to do it? Asians, Latinos, Caucasians, honor students, African Americans, who? You are getting D's maybe C's and you are proud because he has killed you mentally so you wear that D as a badge of honor. "I have passed." Yes, you have passed all right. You have passed on your opportunity to make it to that egg to create new life. You have made it out of the fifth grade; no, you cannot read that well, but at least you have made it. You have passed. Remember my brothers the real reason Pharaoh needed to kill the boys was because he knew a liberator was coming. He knew another Malcolm was coming. He knew another Martin King was coming. He knew another Medgar Evers was coming. He knew another Shaka Zulu was coming. He knew another Steve Bico was coming. He knew another Nelson Mandela was coming, so he has to kill you. Reminds you of the time when Jesus was born. Herod got wind of the fact that the Messiah had been born and an end to his oppressive kingdom was forthcoming. Herod killed all the young boys in Bethlehem trying to crush that liberator.

But Matthew: 2 reports that in order to escape the extermination attempt by Herod, Joseph, Mary and Jesus went into Egypt, Africa. You, too, must go back to Africa, your history, your ancestral accomplishments to escape the modern extermination. Just like Jesus, you must walk with a new level of consciousness because you are the next liberator. I have to tell you something. I do not feel too confident if you are happy with getting C's. I do not feel too confident if all you do is playing PlayStation eight hours a day. You know how to whip somebody on some game. So you brag about being the best at Madden 2K3. Playing games…while you are playing games your counterparts are studying. They are creating the games that you keep buying. Playtime is over. I Corinthians 13:11 reminds us that the great Apostle Paul said that when he was a child he spake as a child; he acted like a child; he walked; he talked like a child; he threw tantrums like a child; and he disrespected his parents like a child. When he became a man, when he completed his rites of passage, he put aside childish things. I am not saying you cannot have fun, but you have to put something on your spirit. There is more for you to do in this world, in this life than to play games, to fail school, to waste your parents' money and to dishonor the blood of your ancestors.

Public Enemy Number One. Review Questions

1. Describe the fertilization process.
2. How many sperm cells are ejaculated into a woman's vagina during sexual intercourse?
3. What happens to a large number of sperm cells?
4. List the cities that the text says the Hebrews built for the Egyptians.
5. List some treasured cities that African American males are building for America.
6. How did Pharoah deal with the Hebrews wisely?
7. How is America dealing with African American males wisely?
8. Discuss a few ways that the event of slavery continues to affect African American males.
9. What is the good news in this text?

Resource Materials:

1. Akbar, Na'im. Breaking the Chains of Psychological Slavery. Tallahassee, FL: Mind Productions & Associates, 1996.
2. _____. Man Know Thyself. Tallahassee, FL. Mind Productions & Assoc.
3. Hutchinson, Earl Ofari. The Assassination of the Black Male Image. New York: Simon & Schuster, 1996.
4. Kunjufu, Jawanza. Countering the Conspiracy to Destroy Black Boys. Chicago, IL. African American Images, 1985, 1986, 1995.
5. Moore, Keith L. The Developing Human: Clinically Oriented Embryology.Philadelphia: Saunders, 1977, 1982, 1988, 1993, 1998.
6. Wilson, Willie F. Releasing the Power Within: The Genius of Jesus Revealed. Washington, DC 1998.

Song of Songs is a true dramatic love song between King Solomon and a Shulamite maiden. It is unfortunate that over the years the Christian church has continued in the false notion that this writing is an allegory for Christ's love for the church. I am of the scholarly opinion that this is a story of one of Solomon's courtships and a picture of how beautiful erotic love is between man and woman when it has time to grow and develop without being tainted by the impurities of the modern world.

"Stop in the Name of Love." Seven Reasons Why Fools Should Not Fall in Love.
Song of Songs 3:1-5

Love is a many-splendored thing. For centuries, people have been writing about it, talking about it, singing about it and experiencing love. There are so many different degrees to love. There are so many different definitions, but this writer of Songs, is talking about erotic love. I do not know if you have ever fallen in love before, but something happens to you when you fall in love. It seems to be factual that men do not fall in love often, but when we do fall, we fall hard. I, myself, have fallen in love one time and that was enough for me. Men used to think those shoes were sharp, but now that you are in love, all she has to say is that she does not like them and they are gone out the window or in the trashcan. Men decide to spend a little money when we fall in love. We start to buy little trinkets just because we care. All of a sudden our voice changes when we answer the telephone. We do not mind holding hands while we walk down the street, when we fall in love. Men and boys fall hard. Before we would say, "Girl, I am not holding your hand." But when we fall in love, it is, "Let us go tip-toeing through the tulips." When we are at work, we write little love notes, when we fall in love. But for women, it is a little different. Women fall in love a little more often than men do.

When women fall in love, I have heard that sometimes they lose their appetite. All of a sudden a size 12 is too big; size six becomes the goal. There is a certain coyness about women when they fall in love. There is a certain look that they give you. When they fall in love, it is almost like they fall out of their mind. Some women used to say, " I will never cook for a man..." until they fell in love. "I am not ironing any man's clothes. He is going to iron his own clothes," before they fell in love. Falling in love is a dangerous thing. It is not something for fools.

Proverbs 12:15 says that a fool is one who trusts in himself and does not adhere to the wisdom of God. Here in modern relationships, we find that a lot of people are falling in love and are not ready for what happens when they fall. We will find today that it is no simple thing to fall in love. When you are in love, your nose is wide open; they tell me, to the point where your nostrils flare so wide that they impede your vision. The first thing I want you to notice about falling in love prematurely comes from verse one of our focal text. The Shulamite woman says that at night, while she is sleeping, she begins to seek in her mind the one her soul loves. Now, young people, all of us have been here before. **Reason Number One**, why fools should not fall in love is a song made famous and sung by The Temptations, called "**Just My Imagination**." The song opens with the words: "Each day through my window I watch her as she passes by. I say to myself, 'You're such a lucky guy. To have a girl like her is truly a dream come true. Out of all the fellows in the world, she belongs to you.'" Then the heart-breaking part comes. "But, it was just my imagination, running away with me." When you fall in love, your imagination starts playing games with you. You think about the person all the time, morning, noon and night. Your books start looking like them. You become so preoccupied that you cannot function logically or rationally. Many times you start looking for something that you should not be looking for and my grandmama used to always say, "Do not go looking for something you cannot handle, if you find it." I am not necessarily saying you, but I am saying those people who fall in love who are fools go searching for stuff. "Whose business card is this? Whose number is this on your phone or in your pager? Who is Daryl Johnson? What is this business card doing in your purse? Or your pants pocket?" But it is just your imagination running away with you. Reason Number One: fools should not fall in love because when you are in love, your imagination starts going crazy. You are not you or in control of you anymore. There are things that you said that you would never do that you are doing now. You are in love; you are young, immature, and not ready. If there was one thing that I could do, it would be to protect my children from falling in love too early. I dread the day when my daughter comes home and says, "Daddy, he broke up with me." It does not matter how many times I have broken up with girls and broken their hearts. I feel for the brother who breaks my little girl's heart.

Your imagination starts floating when you are young and not ready for the erotic and passionate love. Erotic love must be accompanied with divine responsibility because without divine responsibility, when you fall in love, your imagination will cause you to do all kinds of crazy stuff. I do not care how saved you are. Fall in love, then let your "sweet pea" leave you for someone else.... I do not care how many songs you sing in the choir, you might flatten a tire, when you are a fool in love. Love does not care what race you are a part of, what school you go to, or what grade you are in. Love is just love.

In Verse 2 the woman says, "I will now get up." First of all, not only does love make your imagination run, but it will also make you do crazy stuff. In the middle of the night, she says, "I am going to get up out of my bed and go look for the one my soul loves. I do not care if he said that he was tired. I am going to look for him in the city, through the streets and in the squares." **Reason Number Two** why fools should not fall in love is like the song, *Looking for Love in All the Wrong Places, Looking for Love*. Look at where she goes when she falls in love and is not ready for it. She went into the streets, the squares, and the clubs looking for her soul's love. Let me caution the young women. First of all, when you fall in love, you do stuff that the Bible tells you not to do. The Bible says, in Proverbs 18:22, a woman does not have any business seeking anybody. You are not supposed to seek. Now, there is not anything wrong with you being discovered. A mature woman knows how to be discovered, but you are not supposed to go seeking anybody.

She went looking in the street, the city, and the squares. Let me modernize it. She went looking in the clubs, the dances and the movie theaters and these are the wrong places to look for love. You go looking for love in all the wrong places when you are young and in love. Now she has this next part correct. In Verse 2b, she said she sought *him*. A woman sought a man, a male counterpart. It did not say she sought *her,* whom her soul loves. Young folks, there is a big move towards lesbianism in our schools. Somebody has said that it is okay to have an alternate lifestyle, but sin is sin regardless of how you dress it up. She sought a man. You should seek a man (if you are just *going to seek*); or if you are a guy, you should seek a woman. She sought him, but she still sought him in all the wrong places.

Can you imagine two o'clock in the morning, getting up out of your bed, putting your clothes on, and looking for your lover? Do you know how crazy you would look, going looking for him or for her? That is crazy, but love will make you do it. There is nobody who does not have a story to tell of how love made them do something crazy. There are a whole lot of people looking to be loved. They want to be swept off their feet. The problem with being a fool and wanting to get swept off your feet is that the wrong broom may sweep you. Young sisters, there are brothers who are trained to sweep you off your feet. Some brothers sit up at night, drinking ginseng and black coffee, meditating on how to holler at you. You are trying to wait until you get swept off your feet and mess around and be lying at the altar asking God to break the chains because you are a fool in love. Even Diana Ross asked the question, "Why do fools fall in love?" She was onto something.

The text reads, Verse 3, "The watchman found me, as they made their rounds on the city; have you seen the one my heart loves?" Not only does your imagination go crazy. Not only do you get out of order and then start seeking love in all the wrong places. Then you start asking people, like the Chilites, **"Have you seen her? Tell me have you seen her?"** This is Reason **Number Three**. When you are a fool in love, you start asking anybody. What are you doing asking a security guard about your love? This is who she asked. How are you going to ask a security guard at CVS to help you find your true love? You will ask anyone about your love. Daddy, Mama, is this the one for me? Deacon, Deaconess, what do you think about this person? You will ask everyone except the Lord, when you are a fool and you fall in love. Love is a powerful emotion that stirs up all your insides and engulfs your whole being. In fact, Song of Songs 8:6-7 says that Love is as strong as death, strong as the mighty fire and not even water can quench the powers of erotic love. That is powerful, but you already know that. You know how long it took the Lord to mend your broken heart. Men, young and old, I do not care how long you all have been broken up, you had better not see her with another guy. **Reason Number Three**: you start asking people have they seen your boyfriend, your girlfriend, your husband or your wife, when you are a fool in love.

Look at **Reason Number Four**. The story goes forward and the woman says, "Scarcely had I passed the security guard when I found the one my heart loves." I title this one like Peaches' and Herb's old hit **"Reunited and it feels so good**." You see in Chapter two they wanted to get together, but she said, "No." She was playing cat and mouse games. "No. Go home"…a little lemonade on the front porch.

> "No, not yet."
> " I have met your mom and dad."
> "No, not yet."
> "I went to church with you."
> "No, not yet…"

Back in the Old Testament times, men and women were used to waiting for love. Now-a-days, we sing about the love and the sex that has already taken place. That is backwards. Back then they wrote poetry about the anticipation of love. Anticipation…I am ready to throw in my player card and love only you! You are looking forward to something great. When you hook up with the person your soul loves, when you are ready, you get reunited and like Peaches and Herb, it feels so good. Fools should not fall in love because sometimes you will meet that one that you love and you need not reunite with that one. "When I found him, I was reunited."

The Bible says she held him and she would not let go. <u>She left her room. She asked the wrong person, "Have you seen him?" She sought after the one and when she found him, she was so happy that she held him and would not let him go.</u> **Reason Number Five** why fools should not fall in love is given in a song written and performed by the group, Paris. They had the number one hit on the charts, "Can't Let Go." When you are a fool in love, you get possessive to the point where you think that the one you love, you own. I am talking mainly to the brothers now. That is *my* woman, *my* wife. Sometimes you get so possessive to the point of abuse. It is in our history. And now sisters are following the same patterns. "Why is she standing beside him at the altar? She does not have any business praying beside my boyfriend. Why is he singing beside her?" You were saved before you fell in love. Everybody was God's creature. Everybody had his or her own purpose to fulfill in life. Now, because you are a fool that has fallen in love, it is no longer God's man or woman. So you have said, "bye-bye" to God. I know God created him, but God created him for me, or God created her for me. I can take it from here. You get possessive when you are a fool and in love to a point where it can be abusive, mentally, physically, and spiritually because you hold onto your love and you do not want to let go. Erotic love will make you possessive. When the Old Testament writers talked about love, it was human. It was passionate. But, in the New Testament, love changes its meaning because of the example of Jesus Christ. It goes from selfish love to the point that it is a full love and you appreciate everything about the person. It moves to agape love. Let me give you an example. When I first met my wife, I was a fool in love. My wife made the best homemade lemon cake in the world. I became possessive and did not want her to make that cake for any one else. My own mama would ask for a cake and I said, "No…my wife – and I get everything that comes with her, even down to the flour, the sugar, and the vanilla extract." When you are a fool in love you get possessive. It is not about sharing your gifts and talents. It is not about you recognizing the gifts and talents in the one that you love. When you are a fool in love, you forget about that stuff. Their future does not matter to you. You are so possessive that the only thing that matters to you is them catering to your ego, when you are a fool in love. "I held him and would not let go," she said.

She goes on to say after she embraced him that she brought him into her mama's bridal chamber. **Reason Number Six: when you are a fool and in love, you cannot stop them from suggesting like Marvin Gaye's hit, "Let's Get it On."** How are you going to fight against somebody telling you let's get it on when you are in love? You have skipped class, done his homework; changed your wardrobe to suit her taste and cut your friends back. So when he says, "let's get it on," you think you have the power to say, "No"?

Please! Do not deceive yourself. You find yourself sinning and you are getting deeper and deeper into a situation that you cannot handle because all you saw was erotic love. First of all, many times fools in love do not even have their own house. I wish that at 35, when my daughter starts dating, she would tell me that she is dating some guy who does not have a car, a house, a job or business, and most importantly does not love the Lord. Why are you wasting your time? Young people, you find the one you love asking you to get it on and then he'll say, "let's get it on in a car;" or she'll say, "let's get it on in the hallway." Something that God has given you that is so precious – your body – and he has to take you to his mama's house to his room that he grew up in from the time he was a baby? College student, your friend offers to "get it on" and then she has to take you to her dorm, where she cannot even cook you a meal? Her dorm that she does not own, that she had to get a loan for, her dorm? Are you supposed to waste possibly your entire future to go back to a dorm room? But when you are a fool in love, you will do it. Many of us adults can testify.

Fools should not fall in love. She brought him to her mother's house. Now young people, this is a prescription for death. In your mama's house? My mother was quick to tell me, "Boy, if I ever catch you with a woman in my house, if you survive CPR, you had better have your own money, your own home, and pay for your own college education because I am putting you out of here." Praise God, Mama never caught me!

Finally, Verse 5 of this chapter is the **Seventh and final reason**. The Word of God reads, "Daughters and sons of Jerusalem, I beg you. The Word of God is begging you. Everybody, I beg you by the mercies of God, by the does and the gazelles, do not mess with that part of love until you are ready, until it desires. Finally, the text tells us to "Stop in the Name of Love." I know he is everything that you thought you wanted, but stop in the name of love. This is love talking. Love is saying to not mess with me until you are ready for me to be awakened. You are going to start fighting your mama and

your daddy, when you wake me up. Your school is not going to seem important when you wake me up. So, I am begging you, do not wake me up until
you are ready for me to mature.

But you are saying,

> Preacher, I am already in love. I have already fallen in love. My
> heart is *already* broken. I am still mending from the hurt of my
> childhood girlfriend. Or, I am still mending off that brother who
> dated and courted me for two years and now he has left me for
> somebody else. I hear your, Rev. Rudy, but I am still in pain. She
> kept asking me to change, but I did not, so my heart is broken. I
> cannot let him go. I cannot let her go. Is there a word from the
> Lord? I am already there, Rev. Rudy. I wish you had preached this
> one before I fell in love. I was a fool. Is there a word from the Lord?
> Rev. Rudy, I already cannot sleep at night. I already check his caller
> ID and his phone book. Is there a word from the Lord? I hear what
> you are saying, but I'm *already* engaged. I am *already* hooked up.
> How can I not be a fool even though I am in love?

My brothers and sisters, I hear your cries and there is good news found in
the New Testament. John 3:16 reads, "For God so loved the world that He
gave His only son, that whosoever believe in Him shall not perish, but have
ever lasting life." The same way that you applied all that energy to the one
you love, you know when at night you were in bed, seeking and your imagination was running? Now, you have to switch that imagination and that
power. Now, you have to seek the love of God. Now, you have to seek the
love of Christ. The Bible says that God so loved the world that He gave His
only son. That means that love is about the giving process. You have to sacrifice something that is so dear to you. That means you have to be willing to
give up something and if you are young and a fool in love, you are not ready

to give up anything. God said, let me show you how to love. Let me give up of my self. I know you do not deserve it. I know you do not pray like you should. I know that you do not meditate like you should, but I love you even though you do not love yourself. Your bad situation and heartache have awakened my love. You had better look out when something wakes up your understanding of God's love for His children. Some brother or sister has done you wrong, but it has awakened your understanding of the love of God. You are crying now, and especially in the midnight hour, but the Lord is rocking you in the cradle of His arms. Your heart is broken; God's love is everlasting. God's love is eternal. God's love is unconditional. I do not care if he left you for somebody else. All that is going to do is arouse the love of God. The Lord knows how you feel. The Lord knows your heart and your insecurities. God already knows your pain. God already knows your situation. When you lie back in your bed this time seek the love of God. Seek the wisdom of God. Seek the Lord so much to the point that angels will start descending, bringing from above echoes of mercy, whispers of love. All of a sudden, you will rise up out of your bed, but you will not go seeking a man or a woman. You will rise up out of your bed praising God. Your soul will get happy and that is why the songwriter says, "When I think about the goodness of Jesus and all that He has done for me...." I would keep lying in my bed. I would keep lying back, but my soul cries out, "Hallelujah!" You have to seek the Lord. You have to seek the love of God. You have to say, "Lord, I know I put you down for him." "I know I put you to the side for her, but I am sorry, Lord." All of a sudden, you are going to feel the love of Christ. Even though nobody tells you that they love you, the Lord will speak to your ear, "Lo, I am with you even until the end of the world." Just like the Lord loved Peter, even though Peter betrayed Him; the Lord said, "I will be with you. I will restore you." That is the kind of love that Psalms: 51:12 talks about. "Restore unto me the joy of thy salvation."

The Lord knows that you do not know what love is. The Lord knows you are already possessive and abusive. The Lord knows that you are not think-ing about other people, that you are not caring about yourself. But in the midnight hour, you need to ask the Lord to swing low. You need to ask the chariots to swing low. You need to ask the Lord to give you something that helps you to break those chains of possession, that helps you forget about the fact that your imagination is running away with you and ask the Lord to let your imagination run through the Word of God. And when you seek the one that you love, you should ask God first. Then God would send you the one you need to love. I am not saying you cannot like anybody. I am not saying you cannot date. I am not saying that young people and old people do not court, but what I am saying is that when it comes time for you to fall in love, seek the Lord first and let the Lord tell you it is okay to fall in love with this one. Let the Lord give you confirmation in your spirit. Do not listen to what girlfriends and boyfriends tell you. "Girl, I would hold onto him. He is a good man." "Oh, bro she is 'tight.'" No, you let the Lord make that decision. When you seek your true love, what a day it would be, Heaven on earth.

Erotic love is the sweet beckoning call of passion. The best love and the best sex are when your mind is in the mind of God and you know that it is from God. He has given you this erotic love, not to abuse, not to oppress, not to misuse, not to mistrust, but to appreciate God. Older people, I beg you, let our young people see the romantic love in your life. This is your wife. This is your husband. You do not have to be ashamed. You kissed in front of the altar at the church. Our young people need love role models. They need to see what romantic love is all about. You keep talking about do not make this mistake. Do not make that mistake, but you have not shown them how love divinely works. Let them see you. Let them hear you. Knocking on the door... "What are you all doing?" "We are having worship. Stay out and give us a few more minutes. I am meeting the Lord." That is what has happened. We have become so stiff in the church that we are not in touch with our sex-uality and the word even scares you. The young girls feel that their sexuality is their bodies, how big their behinds are, their breasts and their curves because all you tell them is, "Do not wear this. Do not show that." You do not say, "Yes, you are fine, but package it in the right way." This is why the young girls listen to me. I tell them in a minute. "The Lord has blessed you. You have a beautiful body. You are starting to mature. So, do not wear that tight dress. Do not wear that short dress. Do not wear that short shirt that shows your stomach or your navel ring. If that is what you show them [young men], then you speak to the animal in them and that is why you can call them a "dog" because when you are in heat a dog knows. You have to have Holy divine sexuality." We have to teach our young people. So, I beg you young people, stop in the name of love. If you find yourself falling in love, get caller ID. Stop returning phone calls. Change your cell phone number. Switch classes. There is more than one English class. Until you are ready for love, please, do not wake love up.

Stop in the Name of Love. Review Questions

1. Name a few actions that women do when they fall in love.
2. Name a few actions that men do when they fall in love.
3. What is the first reason why fools should not fall in love? Who sang the song? What verse of the text is referenced to the reason?
4. What is the second reason why fools should not fall in love? Who sang the song? What verse of the text is referenced to the reason?
5. What is the third reason why fools should not fall in love? Who sang the song? What verse of the text is referenced to the reason?
6. What is the fourth reason why fools should not fall in love? Who sang the song? What verse of the text is referenced to the reason?
7. What is the fifth reason why fools should not fall in love? Who sang the song? What verse of the text is referenced to the reason?
8. What is the sixth reason why fools should not fall in love? Who sang the song? What verse of the text is referenced to the reason?
9. What is the seventh reason why fools should not fall in love? Who sang the song? What verse of the text is referenced to the reason?

10. What is the New Testament scripture to give comfort to fools who have fallen in love?

Resource:

Turner, Tina. What's Love Got to Do with It?

In these four verses of this the second epistle to Paul's young protégé, Timothy, Paul is admonishing Timothy to be bold and courageous when proclaiming and teaching the Gospel. Scholars agree that Timothy was around 30 years of age and in Greek culture he was considered to be young. Paul assures Timothy that if he walks godly then his youth will not matter in terms of the Gospel of Jesus Christ.

Youth Serving with Power
I Timothy 4:11-16

It is so hard to find good service. It seems as though people have obviously forgotten what it means to serve others. You see this when you go into certain restaurants where there are waiters and waitresses with bad attitudes. They make you wait a little longer to be seated, and then they make you wait a little longer to place your order. You have to wait for the bread, water and then when you finally get what you ordered; in many instances, you get it with a bad attitude.

Many people who serve have not understood what it means to be a true servant and to serve with love. What is more terrible is that there are certain occupations in which people know that the job is to serve, and yet they do it so begrudgingly. They serve as if they do not want to be there. If you are going to work at a fast food restaurant, and you are going to work at the cash register, remember that the first question you are taught in orientation is, "How may I serve you?"

Police officers whose motto is "To Serve and Protect" seem to have forgotten that they have vowed to <u>serve</u> first and then protect the people. It appears that many teachers are no longer serving with power, rather they are serving under the duress of trying to have children pass the Stanford Nine Test. So many, it seems, are no longer concerned with whether our children understand their ABCs or their arithmetic. The only thing they are concerned with is if they can select the correct answer to get an above average score on the SAT.

So many people have missed the power in true service. Doctors, who are called to serve the sick, find it convenient to only give good service to those people with medical insurance. It only seems fitting that they give the best diagnosis to those people from the rural areas or those people with certain income levels. But when those doctors took the Hippocratic oath and when they passed the MCAT tests, they were not asked if they would serve only people with insurance. (Paraphrasing) the question was, "Do you promise to serve, with integrity, everybody who needs help?" It baffles me. People willingly sign up to work at the Department of Motor Vehicles, sign up to help you get your driver's license and give you the most hell in the world. You do not want to put down your Bible. But sometimes you want to say, "Did you wake up this morning and forget that you vowed to serve me?" I did not help determine what occupation you were going to pick. You said you wanted to be a teacher. *You* went to school to be a doctor. *You* decided to be a lawyer. Your job is to serve me.

Sadly, poor service is not limited to the world. There are people in the church who are no longer serving with power. Some deacons no longer want to come in and serve communion and serve the people. Trustees in the church no longer want to count and be righteous stewards. Many have forgotten what serving is. But I remind them that the Pastor asked them to be an official. The Pastor did not force them. They told the Lord, "Send me, I will go." It is not just limited to the church officials. There are ushers in the house of the Lord who have decided that they were not going to deal with people coming through those doors with all different types of attitudes, coming in God's house with all different kinds of motives. Ushers, you are the ones who said that you would rather be a doorkeeper in the house of God. That was your decision. So when I come into the house of God, greet me with the spirit of love and give me a program, would you please?

We have missed the power of true service. Jesus said that on the Day of Judgment, God is going to say, "Come on up my good and faithful servant...." See, service is what gets you a seat in Heaven, not how much chicken you fried on 2nd and 4th Sundays; not how many choir rehearsals you came to, but to whom have you rendered service. How have you served the least of these? Some folk have forgotten how to serve. If God called you out of darkness into the marvelous light, it is your job to serve.

But we cannot fault the membership. Many ministers of the Gospel have forgotten that their job is to serve the people. The body of Christ seems to have forgotten the very important thing that Martha understood that service is divine. We celebrate Mary being at Jesus' feet without crediting Martha for her discipline in serving. I mean the people did have to eat. When you do whatever you do for the Lord, you have to understand that you must do it with excellence because somebody would love to be an usher; but because they are stretched out on their back, they cannot walk. So when you serve God's people, you ought to do it with an attitude of gratitude.

Paul admonishes us to present our bodies as a living sacrifice, Holy and acceptable to God. This is your Holy and acceptable form of service Romans12: 1. So when you sing in the choir, you are serving the people who come into God's house and need to be blessed through song. You are worshiping through the gift that God has given you.

But how do you serve with power in a world where everybody is doing his or her own thing? Paul tells Timothy: Let no one despise how young you are – nobody, not parents, not teachers, nobody. Let nobody despise what you bring to the table. God has blessed you with something. And you ought to walk with your head up because you know God has given you something that nobody else has given to you. The way you learn how to serve with power is to recognize that you have to lift up your own positive self-image.

First, You Have to Know Who You Are. You can serve with power because what you do represents God. But you have to be careful young people. We live in a world where you, as an African American, are taught to hate who you are. You are taught that your eyes are too dark, so put in hazel-colored contacts. Your face is too plain, put in a tongue ring. Your stomach is ugly, so throw on a navel ring. Throw tattoos all over your body. Your hair is too tight; perm it and put all kings of freakish colors in it and change the way you look. Subconsciously, the world is teaching you to hate your very physical existence. I dare say your Africanness. They are teaching you to deny who you are and when you deny who you are and what God has given you, you cannot serve with power. You will let anybody despise your youth if you do not know and value the power that you have as youth.

There are a lot of older people who wish they could have a chance all over again. Some of us wish we could be your age again. If we could be teenagers again, knowing what we know now, we would set this world on fire. But the reality is we were not serious about the Lord, even though we were in church. This is why we preach so hard to you because we recognize the things you could do if you do it with power and the mindset of serving God's creation. Paul tells Timothy, do not let anybody despise your youth. When you have something to say in school, raise your hand and say it. I do not care if the teacher seems not like you. Raise your hand, if you have something to say. You have to be bold. I am not saying be disrespectful. But what I am saying is that there are certain teachers who do not care if you do not know what you need to know. There are certain teachers who think that you are not going to be anything but a nigger or a thug. So they are not going to put in any extra time with you like teachers of old. You have to say, "I do not understand this problem and we are not moving on until you help me. I am somebody. I have value and power!"

You have to lift up your own self-image. You have to walk with your head up. You have to be the one to let the young girls practicing lesbianism know that this is not the righteous way to live. You have to raise God up in your life so the brothers will forget about Mike and want to be like you. The brothers on the street will want to be like you. Sisters, the girls in your school will want to be like you because you reflect power, grace and confidence and you know how to serve with power. You recognize that your job is to help somebody else and not just be selfish or arrogant because you come from a two-parent home, or because you are in church, or because God has brought you to a certain place. Your job is to reach back and help somebody else. Paul says that Timothy should not let anyone talk about him. Do not let anybody call you a youngin'. Do not let anybody call you just a little African child from the ghetto or the suburbs. Paul says, "Timothy, God gave you something. You were blessed with something and all you have to do is walk in it and watch people step back." It was young people in South Africa during Apartheid who said that they were not going to accept the cruelties and injustice of Apartheid, with its oppression and inferior mis-education. They refused to speak a hybrid language called Afrikaans. Young people stormed out of school buildings and they marched. Many of them lost their lives because racist Anglo Saxon police opened fire on them. It was not only the older folk who rebelled, it was young people who said, "I refuse to be a slave." They stood up and faced machine gun fire because they refused to let the European supremacist power structure despise their youth.

Four little girls in Birmingham, Alabama were killed in church because they were not waiting for somebody to take them into the church. They were not waiting for the adults to call a youth pep rally. They were not waiting for the adults to call a youth workshop. They were in the house of God and they lost their lives; but because of their example, you can go and worship freely without the fear of being blown up during altar prayer because of what they did.

During the Montgomery bus boycott, young people helped. It has always been young people. Children walked to school and to the stores with their parents. We need you to know that you have the power. Paul says to Timothy, "First, be an example." Is it not a shame that so many of our people when they are in church they are saved; when they are in the choir, they are singing, "Help me lift up the name of Jesus. I love the Lord;" but then the minute they hit the school system and demons get on them, they do not have enough strength to stand up and fight the enemy? Paul says, you be an example in season and out of season. You walk with your head up. You pull your pants up. You tell somebody how to dress. You be an example in what you are saying, and in how you look. Forget what everybody in the fifth grade is doing and what everybody in the fourth grade is doing. Paul says, "Timothy, you be the example." Grandmama and Granddaddy used to say it this way, "I do not care what they do over there. We do not play that in this household. You have a charge to keep. You have something to do." Your job is to be an example. Paul says, be an example in your speech, in what you say. I get so tired of young folk, in the body of Christ, who still think it is cool to talk ignorantly. Young people, it was a time when your ancestors were stolen from Africa and the slave traders did not teach them the English language. They did not teach them how to speak. By the power of God they learned to read the Bible and figure out English all by themselves. Occasionally, some true Christian European folk would help. You, however, do not have any excuse. Be an example in your speech.

I was watching a documentary on MTV of Tupac Shakur. Many older people do not like Tupac and a lot of people who could not understand him just called him a thug and wrote him off. The video clipping was of a younger Tupac, about 17 or 18. His mother was a Black Panther. So you know Tupac knew a little something. He had a street life, but he also had a Black consciousness. When he was speaking at 17, the boy was speaking like a preacher. His gift of oration was awesome. He asked the person interviewing him, "How in the world could the President, living in the White House with so many empty rooms, have homeless people right in front of the White House, and yet say he is trying to fight homelessness?" And, it hit me real hard. Paul says, Timothy be an example in what you say. Your words can make the world listen. The first thing you need to do is to affirm the power of Jesus Christ in your life. You have to be the one to tell the dying youth that Jesus is alive. Parents, if you knew how our young people are under attack; many or our young people are falling to this lesbian movement and this homosexual movement. It is so awesome with what they face. My young people tell me that lesbians are in schools in gangs busting in the restrooms. Young girls trying to go to the restrooms are being harassed and forced into lesbianism. That is an awesome demon that is in all of the schools. All of our young people are facing it. But we need some young folk who know the power of God and know the power of service that will begin to walk together in Christian gangs and walk up in the restrooms and just be an example of speech and of conduct. Tell them that, "this is God's turf and it is my job to not let a demon in hell despise the power of my youth, or these other youth in school with me." We need young folks to be examples in school.

Everything goes back to serving with Power. Your ancestors died trying to read. They had their hands cut off, their feet cut off and their eyes plucked out because they were trying to learn how to read. Again you do not have any excuses because they paid their life in service. Our slave ancestors gave their blood, sweat, and tears. You have the Internet. You have encyclopedias in your room. You have everything that you need. You have no excuse not to be brilliant.

Now, if you are doing your best and you are studying and you are praying and a C is all you are bringing home, then we will give God the glory for that C. But you have to be an example in conduct. It is not that you cannot learn. Some of you all are just lazy. Some of you know more codes on the PlayStation than you know timetables. You spend all your time playing

PlayStation; you do not have anything in your head. When people come to you looking for a word, you cannot speak with power. You cannot serve with power, but you can play that PlayStation.

You can play it. You can beat anybody on the PlayStation. While you are learning how to play games, the young Asians are making the games that you are spending your parents' money on. Your Asian counterparts know their algebra. They know how to build computers and all you can do is play what they build. And you wonder why people despise your youth? Paul says, "Timothy forget about all of that. I do not care what people say about you. Do not let anybody despise your youth." And one way for you to develop a positive self-image is to be a good example in speech and in conduct.

Then Paul says, in spirit; that means, young folk, you have to have the right spirit. The way you talk to your parents should be different from the way somebody else without the right spirit would talk to their parents. The way that you do your work should be different from the way other people whose spirit is out of sync with the Lord would do their work. The way you take care of your room should be different from somebody who has a spirit of ingratitude. If you only were connected to the fact that your mother and father did not have a bed; if you were connected to the fact that folk all around the world are sleeping on the ground and dying from starvation, being raped and molested; if you were connected to the fact that angels are watching over you and God is protecting you, you will understand that you have to, in spirit, serve with power. Your Christ helps you serve with power. You have to lift up God. You have to lift up the name of Jesus.

It does not take a whole lot, young people. All you have to do is to say, "Jesus." There is power in the name of Jesus. You do not have to pray and hit somebody over the head with a bottle of olive oil. When you are in a bad situation, all you have to do is say, "in the name of Jesus." That is all you have to say. You do not have to fall over backwards. All you have to do is say, "Jesus;" that is all you have to say is "Jesus." Then be an example in faith. I want to know that you should try to start Bible study in your school. You should help the teacher do her job. You ought to be different. Set an example in faith. The story is told of two young girls who had to stay at school late. After they had finished their work, they came out front to wait for their parents. Some men drove up in a car, jumped out the car and snatched them. They took the girls into the woods. The men told the young girls that they were going to rape them and then kill them. They took one in the back seat while the other was in the front. The men began to try to rape her. And then the young girl, the youth in the front, began to call on the name of the Lord. She started saying, "Jesus, I need you. Jesus, help us. Jesus, help us." All of a sudden, the guy in the back looked out the rear window and said to his friend up front, "Do you see that man standing out there with a shot gun?" They stopped what they were doing and put the two girls out and when they sped off there was nobody out there. It was an Angel. It was the Son of God. And if you set the example in faith, the power and presence of God Almighty will come to you. You have to be an example. You cannot let anybody despise your youth. It does not matter how young you are. You lift up the name of Jesus and by faith, you will save your parents. That is why the Bible says that a lion, the king of the jungle and a lamb, the weakest animal will sit together and a youth will lead them. God has given you something.

Not only does Paul say you have to **lift up your own positive self-image**, but then he says you have to *affirm* who you are. You have to look yourself in the mirror and say, "I am a bad African American child of God. My ancestors have endured the horrors of the Middle Passage. Before that, they built the pyramids. They founded math. They founded science. You must be able to say, "There is nothing I cannot do; nothing I cannot learn. I am a child of God. I am the one to be like. If you want to know who to be like, look at me because I am bad. I am the one. Even if I have on K-Mart shoes, I am still bad. If I have on *Jordan's*, I am still bad. What I have on does not make me who I am. For the Lord fashioned me. He breathed into me the breath of life. The most important thing is not how I dress up this body. It also matters that I lift up my spirit unto God." You have to have a positive self-image.

Then Paul tells Timothy not to neglect the gift that is in you. Some elders laid their hands on you and called forth the gift of God that was in you. This gift is not to know how to be a good cheerleader. This gift is not to know how to dress well. It is nothing so superficial. The elders laid their hands on you and called forth the anointing of Jesus. They called forth God in your life. There is something in you; people will try to crush it, young girl. People will try to kill you, brother, but God has blessed you with a spiritual gift. And if you do not use it, nobody else can. Everybody has a gift but not everybody has decided to use that gift. The elders laid their hands on you. Some elder down on their knees said, "I might not be the one to go to college, but in the name of Jesus my seeds will go to college. I might not be the one to learn how to read, but my seeds will learn how to read." They laid their hands on you, even before you were born because they did it in the spirit. They were connected to God in the spirit even though you were unknown to them in the flesh.

If you can just get in touch with being a good server, you will understand that wherever you are going, however you walk, the Lord will make your paths straight and your enemies your foot stool. If you want to serve with power, get in touch with the gift that God has put in your soul. There are going to be some times when you come to your parents and your parents are not going to understand what you are talking about. Your parents are not going to want to hear that foolishness. There is something that God gave you that folks are not going to understand but if you know it God will breath on it and some elder will lay their hands on you in church and say you are going places, you are going to do something. I do not care what the world says about you. I do not care what the media says about you. You are God's child. There is something great in you. When you go to sleep, mama and daddy will come into your room, put olive oil on your head and say, "I call forth God."

There is power. Parents, you ought to serve God by anointing your children's head with oil. Our children are facing too much stuff. Some stuff they alone cannot battle in their spirit. They need to know that you are praying for them. Before they leave the ark of safety, called your home, in the morning you ought to place God's anointing on their heads so that they will walk out knowing that they are bad and feeling that the blood of Jesus covers them. If you get that combination going your child will reach higher heights.

Paul tells Timothy, **do not neglect that gift**. Do not let anybody quench your spirit, young people. You are going to go places. You are going to find some teachers who do not like you. They do not like your mama. They do not like your daddy. They do not like the fact that you are saved. They just do not like you. They do not like you because you are African American. Some are not going to like you because you have cornrows or dreadlocks but forget about that. Do not neglect your gift. Speak truth to power. That which God has given you, folk will have to recognize it. Once you hold your head up and say, "This is where I am going;" folk will sit back and recognize what God has given you. And then you can serve your peers. You can serve them with power.

Let me tell you a story. My pastor, Rev. Willie F. Wilson, was running for mayor of Washington, DC in 2002. During the campaign I saw this young guy, 11 years old, had a suit on, I said, "Here man, help pass out some flyers." He said, "No." Being from the old school, I was about to knock his head off because I do not play young folk telling me what they are not going to do. He came back and said, "I am training for security." He made me step back and look at him because he was serious. He did not crack a smile. He said, "I am training to be a security person." I started watching him and watching how he was walking. He was following the other security people. He was walking behind the pastor and I said, "Yes, you are training to be security. Excuse me for trying to take away your gift."

Folk will recognize if you know what you are doing. Just be who God created you to be and watch how people step back. They will step back from you. Do not neglect the gift that is inside of you because somebody paid his or her life for you to step up. Some ancestor was hung from a tree so that you could be here. Brothers, some father with your genes was castrated so that you could be here. Young girl, some mother was raped so that you would not have to be a whore voluntarily. African women were raped every night but because they knew that the time would come where you would be able to make the wise decision to keep your chastity they were able to endure. You dare not disrespect what they went through. Your job is to serve your ancestors with power and thank them for their struggle.

Finally, Paul says, "Timothy build up your self-image and do not let anybody despise your youth; once you understand your gift, do not let anybody neglect your gift." Then he says, "Just watch what you do. If you keep these things, you Timothy, *one person*, you will **Save yourself and everybody who hears you**. That is the power of serving. When you serve in the right spirit, when you serve under the Lord Jesus Christ, when you give God the glory for what you have; not only will you be saved, but also everybody who hears you will be saved. All you have to do is know that the word of God says that if you lift up Jesus, you will save the people around you. You know what this means? This means everybody in the fourth grade shall be saved when you lift up Jesus. Everybody in the sixth grade shall be saved. Everybody who hears your voice in your household will be saved. You know why? Because now you understand how to serve with power and because you know who you are and whose you are, when you speak people will have to listen. When you open your mouth, folk have to pay attention. When you walk places, folk have to check you out. When you do things, folk have to stop and see what you have. When they see what you have, you point them to the cross and you point them to Jesus. I hear the Lord saying, "Come unto me; all ye that labor and are heavy laden and I will give you rest." You lift the Savior up higher, higher, and watch those lesbians straighten up. Watch the drug users stop smoking. All you have to do is lift up the name of Jesus because there is power in your service, power in your body, power in your soul. You are a great people. You can do great things, but first be a good example and lift up Jesus. Lifting up Jesus means telling people you know who is responsible for your life and everything that you have. Lifting up Jesus means when you are confronted with people saying it is okay to smoke or be gay or not do your best, you can refute these claims by affirming that greater is He that is in me than he that is in the world. You lift up Jesus by telling them that these alternate social deviations are unacceptable in the eyes of your Savior. You lift Him up. The Bible says I will draw all men and women unto me. Lift the Savior up for the world to see. For the world is hungry for the Living Bread. Be a good example. Walk like you have the power to serve. Talk like you have the power to serve. Be who you are because you are who God created you to be. And what God created nobody else can add to it. We can only help you to get there, but you are all put together.

For the Bible says that after God had created everything He created, He rested. That means He did not do any more work. That means everything that you need is already in you. You are praying to be in tune with the power. So that is how you learn to serve and if you understand true service, true worship, you not only save yourself, you save everybody that the Lord allows to come into contact with you.

Youth Serving with Power. Review Questions

1. What age was Timothy when the Apostle Paul wrote him this letter?
2. Cite three examples of people in the world who offer poor service.
3. Cite three examples of people in the church who offer poor service.
4. What is the power of true service?
5. List and explain the first step in learning how to serve with power.
6. List and explain the second step in learning how to serve with power.
7. List and explain the third step in learning how to serve with power.
8. List two consequences the African American slaves experienced when they were caught trying to read.
9. Describe two events in African and or African American history when youth led the way.

Resources:

1. Davis, Kortright. Serving with Power: Reviving the Spirit of Christian Ministry New York: Paulist Press, 1999.
2. James, George G.M. Stolen Legacy. Newport News, VA: United Brothers Communications Systems, 1989.
3. Mathabane, Mark. Kaffir Boy in America: An Encounter with Apartheid New York: Scribner, 1989.
4. Lee, Spike. Documentary: Four Little Girls.

This parable taught by Jesus seems to picture God as actively seeking sinners and those who are lost. The Lost Sheep parable is the first of the three covering this subject matter. The other two are the Lost Coin and the Prodigal Son.

The Power and Value of One
Luke 15:2-7

We live in a world today where much emphasis is placed on quantity. Society has led us to believe that the power is in numbers and not in the quality. This psychological conditioning persuades us to become involved with packs, gangs and numbers of folks to establish an identity because we no longer feel that there is power/value or uniqueness in one.

Try and tell someone that you only have one savings or checking account and they may criticize you and question your financial stewardship. They probably will not consider the possibility that the one savings account could have thousands or millions of dollars in it because all they heard was "one." It really does not matter what happens after you say "one." Most folk are turned off when you tell them you only have one. Something about one just is not impressive anymore here in America. Young folk tell you that on their report card they have one A and parents and guardians may begin fussing at your apathetic attitude towards school or start complaining about how much money you are costing them, and they ignore the possibility that you may have seven A+s because all they heard was "one."

One has lost its power here in North America. We have been inundated with numbers. How many do you have? How many times have you done it?

It is paramount that we understand that one or one time is significant. It only takes one sexual experience to get HIV or become pregnant. It only takes one extra hit of cocaine to overdose and die. It only takes one time for you to get arrested and put away for 20 years, so one is powerful. There is power in one. One young man who decides to walk with his head up can change the attitude of the entire class. You have that power. You must understand that you are unique. You are special. There is something about you and you alone; not your sister, not your brother, not your mother, but you all by yourself. God has put the entire kingdom within you (Luke 17:21). God has put the power in you that can change the environment everywhere you go.

Equally, a negative one can have the same adverse effect on the environment. It only takes one child acting like a hoodlum to disturb the whole class. It only takes one person talking in the movie-theater to get you to lose your mind. It only takes one. Adults, it only takes one person cutting you off in the morning. One person looking at you the wrong way and you are subject to lose your religion.

This parable is all about the one. It is talking about the power and value of one. This shepherd has a hundred sheep and one goes astray.

I think it is appropriate to have a few moments of discussion centered on why that one sheep actually went astray. What is it about that one sheep that made it decide to leave the 99? As I was looking at this text, the Lord showed me that maybe the shepherd drove that sheep away. The sheep responds to the shepherd because sheep are the dumbest animals in the world. They cannot even drink water without the shepherd. If they do not hear the shepherd's voice, the sheep will go astray. Maybe the shepherds are driving our young sheep away. Maybe they are not preaching to our youth. Maybe the shepherds are not saying anything in their messages that lead the sheep to the living water for their thirsty souls.

A second possibility is that the herd drove the sheep away. Unfortunately, as it relates to our troubled and misguided youth, we see the

Christian community do this a lot of times. Young people who have been called whores, thugs and niggers finally receive an invite to God's house and in God's house, God showed them that they are somebody. God showed them that they are special and they come into God's house into the fold with the other sheep and the fold drives them away because their reputation precedes them. "Oh, your name is Tanya, I heard about you." Your reputation precedes you. The herd, possibly, is driving that one sheep away. A third theory is maybe that one sheep was just a little more unique than the other 99. Maybe that one sheep was more individual than the 99. Maybe that one sheep had something different from the other 99.

Who is to say how that one sheep thought? It is possible that God gave him something special that the 99 did not have

Well, let us stop speculating. This parable Jesus tells does not deal with what drove the sheep away. It only talks about the fact that the sheep was driven away. He was gone. So many of our peers have strayed away from the Good Shepherd, Jesus Christ. They represent the one. They are written off. Your brother is the one. Your "dog" is the one. Your sister-friend is the one. She is driven away and she would be lost without the shepherd coming to get her. One is lost. There is so much power in that one. Who is to say what that one person will do? Who can predict the divine value of that one? Forget what the news and society say about your lost friends. You have the power to persuade that one to come back to the fold.

We must examine what qualities the shepherd had to possess in order to recover the lost sheep. The shepherd first of all had to **Be Affirming** to the one sheep. The shepherd goes after the one sheep. He forgets about the 99. He recognizes that the one sheep is so valuable that he had to forget what he presently possessed to retrieve the one. He did not know what it could become. The one sheep, adults; that one child who is acting like he is mentally deformed now, might become the next rocket scientist. But, who will ever know if you do not go after the one. The one child that is in special education right now may be the very one who discovers the cure for cancer. Nobody knows if the shepherd does not go after the one. We know we are going to lose some sheep but it is not for us to decide which sheep gets lost. Our job is to understand that God is in control and we ought to <u>affirm</u> the value in all of the sheep.

The second quality of the shepherd is that he was faithful. The shepherd did not say, "Well, I had 100, now I have 99. Let me just work with the 99." The shepherd's job was to go after every sheep at the end of the day. The shepherd had to count his sheep and if he did not have the same number of sheep at the end of the day that he had at the beginning, he had to go find the one that was lost. Like the shepherd, young people, you must **Be Faithful** over what you have. You must live and practice good stewardship. I always try and encourage you young people by reminding you that you are a blessed generation. You have more stuff than your parents ever had. You have a computer in your room and you have your own phone line. You have things that people have never had and you do not take care of them. Young brothers, you have to be faithful over what you have right now. It should be school. If you are doing badly in your schoolwork, deal with the situation. Deal with the one class that you are getting a D in presently. Deal with the one class that you are getting a C in presently. Deal with that one class and all the other classes will fall in place. If that shepherd ignores that one and forgets about the one the next day will come. He will say, "I have 99." Then he may lose another. When the next day comes, he will say that he has 98. Then the next day will come. He will say that he has 97 because he is practicing poor stewardship. He is not being faithful. Before you know it, his 99 may be lost. Brothers, how many brothers do you hang out with who do not attend church? One invitation from you may get them to come. You see, your boys tell you that they are not with that "church thing." But you are the one to change their mind. You might say there is a whole lot of power up in this church thing. There is a lot of salvation up in this church thing and because you say one word to that one brother, you may make the difference. Let me give you an example. Have you ever been in love young people or found a guy or girl you really liked? Brothers, you saw her and you said, "Man she's phat." She looks nice. She's thick. Man, if I could just get one number. "Girl, give me six and let me guess the other one." You feel confident that you may be in the game if she gives you one number out of ten. The older teens would say, "If I could get just one date, one phone conversation, one walk to the locker, one good look. I mean if she looks at me one time, I got her." But it all starts with one. "If I can get the one cornrow style, then I will be the man. If I can just hit the one shot, then I will be the man." Young girls, you say, "If I can turn down the most popular guy in the school one time, then I will be the one." Let me be the one, but you have to be faithful over what God has given you. Look at what you have. Number one, you have shoes and that is more than most young folk ever have growing up. My Uncle Clarence, in Charlotte, North Carolina, will tell you war stories of how he walked in Vietnam without shoes. But you all have shoes. Be faithful over what you have. Some of you all do not take care of your own shoes because they are not $200 *TMACS*, or *Iversons*, or *Air Jordans*, but these people do not care anything about you. You do not take care of the one chain you have, the one pair of shoes you have, the one shirt you have, the one pair of pants you have, the one pair of jeans you have because you do not like it, because you did not want it. If you are not faithful over the one, then God will not bless you with more. In this parable, the shepherd reminds us to be faithful over what you have.

Going after the one sheep, the shepherd says you have to be affirming. Young folks, one mother knelt down at the altar and asked the Lord to bless you and bring you back home. One person lifted your name up before the Lord and you are the result of that one prayer. You are the most powerful, beautiful descendants of African kings, queens, elders, and tribe leaders that will ever be. You are the one generation that will liberate our people. It is you. You are the one, but you will never be the leaders that you were called to be if you continue to play all the time. You watch too much TV. You play too many games. There is so much power in you that everybody in the world is trying to make you think that you do not have any power. The deception is to make you hate who you are. If they can make you hate your culture, hate your history, hate what God has given you, then they have already assured that you will get lost and not be recovered. You have so much power in you that if you walk with your head up; you are the one who will change the way everybody thinks about the church and your generation. One sermon will change somebody's life. One song, one prayer, calling on God's name one time summons the angelic host. You have to affirm who you are. "Affirm" just means looking at yourself in the mirror and saying with all manner of power that, "I am somebody. I am power. I am a King. I am a Queen. I can do it. I can make it." If you do that, you will leave your house feeling like you are on top of the world. You have to tell yourself that. Then you have to tell yourself that the shepherd is coming after you. The shepherd is following you. There are a lot of people who do not like you, but do not let that scare you. There are a lot of educational systems that seek to dethrone you and relegate you to "your place." So what, just focus on the fact that you are the one person and with what God has put in you, you can do great things. Affirm who you are. Love who you are. And know that you have power.

Third, the shepherd teaches us to **Be Trusting** of God. The shepherd said, "I will go after the one. I have to trust that God will take care of the 99 that are left." What I am telling you is not to worry about all the other odds and ends. God has that. God has you, brothers and sisters. You just do your job. Let God do His job. Do not worry about the 99. Go after the one. Be the one. Be the man. One man said he was coming back from retirement and stocks shot through the roof, Michael Jordan. It only takes one. There were a whole lot of children in Egypt, but Moses was the one chosen to liberate Israel. It only takes one. Elijah fought the prophets. There were 350 false prophets, but there was only one prophet of God. It only takes one. There were a whole lot of people with the name "Jesus" born in the first century, but there was only one Savior named Jesus the Christ who was born, who can redeem your soul. It only takes one. The one is powerful. Young people, the one can make a difference but you have to believe it. You have to take care of what you have. I do not care how little you think it is. I do not care how cheap you think it is. Know that your mother and your father are working hard to buy you what they can. If they cannot afford Jordan's, please understand that whatever they give you is given in love and it is a sacrifice. You do God a disservice when you frown your face up over something that your parents buy for you. They worked hard to provide for you and you turn your nose up. That breaks your mother's heart. You do not know how many grandmothers and grandfathers had to struggle and sacrifice to buy you one pair of shoes. You have to understand that it only takes one time of you frowning your face up that can change the relationship between you and your family. The most important thing that matters is not what you wear. What matters is your attitude about the way you are because God cares about what is in you. What you have on the outside is secondary. Your body is developing, that is secondary. You should not get distracted when somebody gets attracted to you because of your physical presentation. This is a minor aspect of who you are. Do not allow that aspect to control you. You must know that you have so much more to offer. There are so many parts of who you are aside from your body, your intelligence, your personality, your belief systems etc. One sheep. The power of one, the one shepherd, the one sheep, the one brother.... Young ladies, it will only take you one time to say, "No." the right way. It only takes one time.

For some of you who grew up in my generation, it only takes one look from your parents, one look for you to straighten up. It only takes one beating and you are all right for the rest of your life, if you have parents from the South, and if you know what is right. It only takes one time of them swinging that belt for you to get a good holler. "Have mercy on me!" Young folk, I want you to know that the Good Shepherd cares about you. I do not care how much the movies degrade you. I do not care how much the media and the Rap stars make you think that all you have going for you are rapping, wearing platinum, Ice, and all the fineries. I do not care how much they tell you that you are never going to be anything. It only takes you believing one time that God is on your side and that God is all power. If you can believe in the one God and the one life He has given, you will make a world of difference in other people's lives. Then you will be able to say, when you go to sleep at night, that you made a difference. First, you made it to yourself. Then you made it everywhere you went. It only takes one song, which you sing in the choir, to save somebody's soul in the congregation. It only takes one. I can be sitting down in church, looking at the choir singing and if my eye catches one person who looks like she really believes what she is singing, the Spirit will fall fresh upon me. It only takes one. I am here to give you power, to let you know that you are children of God, sons and daughters of the Most High, inheritors of the throne. You have a father who is so popular; you have a father who is bigger than any music star, athlete or movie star. You have one heavenly daddy. You should walk with your head up so high because of who your daddy is. People think that I am crazy because I walk around like I actually have a lot of money, but it is because of who my daddy is. He has more money than Fort Knox, more money than Wall Street, more money than any doctor or lawyer you can think of and I walk with my head held up.

You can call me whatever you want to call me, but I have power because I am one person anointed by God to teach one message. When I teach, you are only hearing one teacher; you are seeing one God come through this one teacher. The same thing happens when you open your mouth. One word can bring somebody to church. One word can help your brother pull his pants up on of his behind. One word, sisters, can help you make that boy turn into a gentleman. He can curse around you one time and the way you look at him will make sure he never curses around you again. You mess around and talk back to your mother one time and you may not see another day. There is power in one.

The Power and Value of One. Review Questions

1. What does the parable of the lost sheep picture God as actively doing?
2. What are the two other parables associated with the lost sheep?
3. Where in Luke's Gospel does Jesus inform us that the kingdom of God is within? Give chapter and verse.
4. What are the three reasons the author gives as to why the lost sheep could have possibly strayed?
5. The first action the shepherd had to take to recover the sheep was to be _____.
6. The second action that the shepherd had to take to recover the sheep was to be _____.
7. The third action that the shepherd had to take to recover the sheep was to be _____.
8. How do sheep get to still waters to drink?
9. The shepherd is a poor financial steward if he does not go after the one sheep. What action does this fall under?
10. Leaving the 99 and going after the one lost sheep falls under what action by the shepherd?

Resources

Angelou, Maya. I Know Why the Caged Bird Sings. N.Y.: Bantam Books, 1971, 1993.
1. _____. Still I Rise, New York: Random House, 1978.
2. Diop, Cheikh Anta. The African Origin of Civilization: Myth or Reality. New York. L. Hill, 1974.
3. Haley, Alex. Autobiography of Malcolm X. New York: Ballantine Books, 1965, 1973.
4. James, George G. M. Stolen Legacy. Newport News, VA: United Brothers. Communications Systems, 1954, 1989.
5. King, Martin Luther. Strength to Love. Philadelphia, PA: Fortress Press, 1963.
6. Shange, Ntozake. For Colored Girls Who Have Considered Suicide, When the Rainbow is Enuf: a Choreopoem. New York: MacMillan, 1977.

The Epistle to Hebrews is written to a body of believers undergoing persecution because of their faith in Jesus Christ. They were being burned at the stake and attacked in public arenas by lions to the cheer of angry crowds as were many first century followers of Jesus Christ. Believers before being destroyed were given the chance to turn away from their convictions and be saved physically or they would be killed as martyrs. We owe a lot to the faith of these witnesses who counted it a joy to suffer for the cause of Christ. Chapter 12 then serves as a crucial transition between the witnesses of Hebrews 10:19 and the deceased people of faith in Chapter 11. This chapter and these verses give witness to the blessings of living by faith.

We Have You Surrounded, Come Out with Your Hands Up
Hebrews 12:1-3

I am sure you have seen movies and TV shows where someone has committed some sort of crime a bank robbery, for example. Inevitably, the criminals would barricade themselves inside the bank and start making all kinds of demands. Almost instantaneously, numerous police officers would appear on the scene. The one in charge says on the bullhorn, "We have you surrounded, come out with your hands up." If you are of visible African descent and have ever been pulled over while driving, I am sure you can bear witness to your involuntary participation in a real-life routine traffic stop that ended in some officer calling in reinforcements. Suddenly, five or six police are surrounding you and you hear, "Get out of the vehicle slowly with your hands up, we have you surrounded." Thank God, this is not the admonition to which this writer of the 12th chapter of Hebrews is speaking. This writer is saying that you are surrounded, young people by ancestors, elders and adults who have witnessed to the faith of Jesus Christ. These are adults who have been there where you are, who have endured the different hardships and trials that you have gone through and are now surrounding you with prayer, surrounding you with their testimony and surrounding you by their witness.

I know you are surrounded by racism, although sadly, America and your own people deny it. I know you are surrounded by sexism. I know you are surrounded by educational discrimination where you still pledge allegiance to a flag representative of people who hate you and refuse to include you in the annals of history. I know you are surrounded by poverty. I know you are surrounded by misguided and immoral peers who practice sexual perversion, smoke marijuana etc., but these are not the type of witnesses to which Hebrews refers. This writer is talking about the witnesses in the biblical record who have gone on by faith to do great things for God and for their people. It talks about Abel offering a better sacrifice than Cain, Enoch and Noah, and Abraham and Sarah, Jacob, Moses and even Rahab the harlot. This writer is telling you to look around you and see the witnesses who have done great things in the name of Jesus Christ. I know you are 13, 14, and 15 now. I know that you know everything that is going on in the world now. I know you have your own phone and you can do it for yourself. I know you are a straight A student but the writer is telling you to hold up. Some people who know a little more than you know surround you.

I know you are reaching puberty. I know you are beginning to develop and you are beginning to smell yourself a little bit. (That's the old folks' saying for thinking that you are all of that). But please understand that you do not know what you need to know about your body and about life. You do not know what it is to walk this road of life yet. All you know is the fact that you have three squares and somewhere to lay your head so you had better look to the people who are surrounding you. This writer is talking about you not forgetting about those people who paved the way for you. You can forget about the cops, the media, and those people who do not like the way you wear your hair or the language that you speak. But do not forget about your ancestral witnesses.

Young people, many of you are not confident in yourselves because many of you are not connected to God and to your history. It is impossible for you to stand firm in the face of adversity without being connected to God. As we look at this text, God seems to show us three very simple steps to take in order to get connected to the power of God thereby tapping into the faith of the witnesses surrounding us.

The first step is found in verse 1: therefore, we are also surrounded by a great cloud of witnesses. The Lord is saying first of all look at who you are surrounded by, young people. Look at your peers. How do they think? Are they trying to get you to skip school? Well then, some misguided people surround you. Young ladies, are those surrounding you trying to get you to sleep with everybody you can, singing and embracing songs like Lil' Kim talking about, "How many licks does it take you to get to the middle of it?" If so, then you are surrounded by peers who do not love themselves and only see themselves as animals who cannot control their own minds and bodies. You had better look at who is surrounding you. Do people who curse out their teachers and do not do their work and then blame the school system surround you? The writer says look at who is surrounding you. Check out their actions. The mouth will say anything but behavior will not lie. They can tell you that they love you all they want but if they try to get you to smoke a blunt, or become a lesbian, or homosexual, or play games all day long, they do not love you and they do not love themselves. You had better look at the witnesses who are walking with you. Yes brothers, your Dogs, check them out. Check out their grade point averages. If people with a 1.5 or a 1.8 grade point average surround you and they say that they are doing well, you had better get up out of their company.

If brothers are talking about how many girls they have slept with, then somebody who does not care about his own people surrounds you. Young sisters, who is surrounding you? What are they talking about all the time? What is the dominant conversation around these people? When you see them in the hallway, what are they talking about? Are they talking about preparing for school? Are they talking about moving forward? Are they talking about something righteous? Are they talking about rebuilding the African American nation? Listen to what they are saying.

The first way you get connected is to **look at who is around you**. Then you can see who you have to let go. When I went to school, I was hanging around with some guys who were not going to the type of school I was attending. I was going to a college high school. I was surrounded by some folk who were going to public school. There is nothing wrong with public school, but they were not going to any school. When I left school I would hang out with them on the street. They did not have the same kind of work-load I had because they were not going to school. For me to get a C and them to get an F was all right. No. No. No, that was not happening. My mama said very clearly, "Boy, this school costs too much money. C's are unacceptable."

The next step the writer of Hebrews shows us, after you look at the witnesses surrounding you, is to lay aside every weight and the sin that so easily catches us up or knocks us off course, if you will. The second thing you have to do, young folk, is you have to **lose some weight**. Some of you young folk are out of shape. Physically, you have to lose some weight. Your diets are terrible. You eat anything you want to eat. The media reports the danger of mad cow disease and the germs that are in the meat, put it right there in front of us, and we still run to McDonald's and "super size" the fries and gulp down the Big Mac. It does not make sense. We have to lose some physical weight. You have to watch what you eat. Some of the stuff you eat is affecting your spirit and your mind. You know the old saying, "You are what you eat"? Well, that is true, because if all you eat is junk food then you are going to have a junk mind, a junk spirit, and you are going to have junkie actions. We have to lose some weight young people. Some of you all are out of shape. You might be one of them. You have to lose some weight. You have to watch what you eat. Drink some more water. Put those sodas down. When you all are in school and experts say that you are too hyper and cannot learn, it is because you are doped up with all kinds of sugar that have you bouncing off the walls. I guess you cannot learn math. Your brain is racing 100 miles an hour. The chemicals and steroids in the food you eat are affecting your natural divine ability to process coherent thoughts and simple logic patterns.

Then we have to lose some mental weight. Young folk, you had better stop tripping off of who does not like you. You had better stop tripping off of what they say about you because what they say about you is none of your business. Do not trip off of what they think about you because number one: most of them do not like you anyway. The media does not like you. Other races, most of them, do not like you. They think that you are little Negro children and you do not have any value. Forget about them. Lose that mental weight. Stop thinking that getting a C: is all right. Forget about that. That is gone. That is mental weight. That thing is bearing you down, brother. God is calling you to a high academic level so you can be on a new level. You had better forget that stuff. Shed that old lazy attitude. I was talking to my daughter, Imani, one day because she told the teachers that sometimes she used to think about running away at eight years old because she had chores. I had to minister to her. My wife takes the sympathetic approach. That is why God put us together but I do not take that approach because she has to lose some mental weight. As hard as I work and with all that she has, I told her that all I have to do is to take away some of the things that she has and she will not have to worry about responsibility at 10 years old. But if the Lord blesses you with something, you have to work for it. She has to lose some mental weight. I told her something else. I said, "Listen, I love you to death. I have to tell you this. But if you want to go away, your mother and I will take our time and pack up everything you brought into the world and ship you wherever you want to go." Young folk you have everything that you need to be an A student. Some of you have Internet in your room. You have full access to the Internet and yet you surf all kinds of stupid chat rooms while your grades are suffering. The witnesses that are surrounding you are those who have died and fought for freedom, those who have been burned at the stake, those people whose hands were cut off for reading just so they could pass down through their genes some semblance of education – and all you are doing is playing games? You have to lose that weight. This life is not about playing games. This life is not about just having a good time. If all you want is to have a good time, go to the Bahamas somewhere, but right here you have to do the Lord's work.

Then you have to lose some spiritual weight. You have to shed some of that guilt. I am talking to the adults now. Adults, some of us are so burdened down with spiritual weight that we put up a block or hindrance with our young people. This is where the generational gap comes into play. Our young people are developing quickly, fathers and mothers. Now you see she has buttocks, hips, and breasts, and it scares you to death because you remember how it was when you began to mature. That thing takes you back to the 50s, 60s and 70s and you say, "Oh my God." It scares you to death. No, you have to shed that stuff. Brothers, you have to shed that stuff. You know the saying that you were going to have some daughters some day so it can come back on you. All those sisters you have run with, all those hearts you have broken, you had better shed that stuff because it blocks you from talking to your daughters and to your sons about sex. You have to shed that spiritual weight. That stuff is heavy. That stuff blocks your connection. Some of this stuff we have learned, we have to unlearn, even in the church. Some of this old stiff, stuck, Christian tradition is continuing to kill our children and force them to run into the street. We have to lose that stuff. That stuff is not righteous. The European slave masters taught half of that stuff and we keep preaching it today. Ministers are preaching the same words that the head preachers on the plantation were preaching. We have to lose it. Our young folk need to be liberated, empowered, and educated. To get connected you have to lose some weight.

Then finally, the word says you have to look unto Jesus, Hebrews 12:2. "Looking unto Jesus, the author and finisher of our faith, for the joy that was set before him endured the cross despised in the shame and now sit down at the right hand of the throne of God." First you have to know what Jesus did. This writer is letting us know in Hebrews that Jesus came from glory to earth so that He could bring us back to God; so that He could connect us back to God. Jesus was the perfect sacrifice. Look unto Jesus who endured the shame. He died like a criminal so that we could be free. He died like a thug who was against the Roman government just so we can say, "Yes, Jesus lives and because He lives I can face tomorrow." Look unto Jesus who saw God and forgot about what he was dealing with. I know you have a low grade point average now but that is right now. You continue to look around you. You continue to look at Jesus and see how Jesus walked by faith. Maybe this is why the writer opens Chapter 11 up with the Bible's only definition of faith as the substance of things hoped for, the evidence of things not seen. Then this eleventh chapter goes on to give us all of these biblical witnesses by faith. Abraham, who did not believe God could do it, stepped up and showed faith and now he is counted as a friend to God. Sarah who was a million years old believed God and then had a child. Noah, who believed God, was saved from the flood. You see, by faith Moses stood at the Red Sea and parted the waters. By faith the children came up out of Israel. These are the witnesses that surround you. So when you get connected, when you look at who is around you, when you lose some weight then you have to look to

Jesus. And when you look to Jesus you live by faith. By faith, you will be the first African American child to move your family out of the ghetto. By faith, you will be the first African American child to graduate from college. By faith in your family, you will be the one who brings your parents back together. By faith, you will be the one to stop somebody from shooting somebody else.

By faith, when you look to Jesus, when you are connected to God, demons will flee. By faith, that young brother who is trying to make you his conquest, God will tell him to back up off of you. By faith, brothers, when racism comes your way you can look racism in the face and say, "I am somebody." By faith, when you are connected, you can go to that teacher who does not like you and say, "I do not care what you think about me. I am God's child." By faith, you can do it. By faith, you can make it. By faith, you have the power. You have to know you have the power and by faith, you can do great things. Those witnesses...you have some unseen witnesses around you. You have some fathers and mothers on the slave ships, who said, "Before I will be a slave, I will be buried in my grave." They sent that spirit down generations so that you have inside of you the power to stand up to people who do not like you. You have it inside your blood. You are surrounded, brothers, by men who looked that slave master in the face and said, "I came from Africa the cradle of civilization. I came from kings. I came from queens. I came from a rich legacy and I do not care if you do not put my history in the book. I know I am somebody." By faith, you can do it and by faith, you can make it.

We Have You Surrounded, Come Out with Your Hands Up. Review Questions

1. How does Hebrews: 11 define faith?
2. List three areas the author says currently surrounds young people?
3. What does it mean when adults say that you are "smelling yourself"?
4. Why are so many young people not confident in themselves?
5. What is the first thing you have to do to get connected to the power of God?
6. What is the second thing that you have to do to get connected to the power of God?
7. What are three different types of weight that you have to lose?
8. What is the third step in getting connected to the power of God?

Genesis 4 records the story of the birth of Cain and Abel as well as the murder of Abel by his brother Cain. It is in this chapter that we are introduced to sexual intercourse between Adam and Eve for the first time. In addition, the focal text seems to show us the consequences of acceptable and unacceptable offerings to our God.

Don't Do the Crime,
If You Can't Do the Time.
Genesis: 4

There used to be a television show in the late 60s early 70s, that I watched at night while growing up, called Baretta. The theme music opened with the words, "Don't do the crime if you can't do the time. No. No." The background would come in, "Don't do it." I liked Baretta because he made it a point when he locked up the criminals, the bad guys, to tell them that, "You are going to jail now, but you should have considered your punishment before you committed the crime." And when we look at today's young people and their parents we are doing a lot of crimes in the house of God, but we are not really prepared for the punishment that God has been laid out for us. Many people consider some possible consequences but we never really fully consider the punishment that could happen.

You see, what happens is before you decide to do a crime you should consider what could possibly happen to you. After you do the crime the thing that you thought would happen does not necessarily happen that way. So you are planning that maybe I will get yelled at or that mama will just take the

PlayStation. What you failed to realize and what you found at the crime scene is that your mother would not only take the PlayStation, but you would also lose her trust. She beats the devil out of you and then you go a long time trying to get back into her favor, but you never thought about that. You only thought about the crime. The story about Cain and Abel let's us know that you ought not do the crime and then go crying to God because you cannot do the time that comes with that crime.

I found that we are committing serious crimes even in the church. Our young people are doing the crimes of desecrating their bodies, their temples. They are eating anything, carry-out french fries, steak and cheese, mumbo sauce, fish and cheese. We are loading them up on McDonald's Mc-ribs, Big Mac, filet-o-fish, Popeye's chicken, mashed potatoes, red beans and rice and washing it all down with cold Coca-Cola. We're doing the crime to our bodies but we are not ready to take on the punishment of hardened arteries, and the punishment of obesity and diabetes, the punishment of falling out, and the punishment of heart attack. We are doing the crime at the table. But when the doctor comes and tells us that our young person, at 13, has to take insulin for the rest of his life, his body riddled with diabetes, we call out to the Lord. My punishment is more that I can bear!

We are doing educational crimes, young people. We are spending more time in front of the television. We are spending more time focusing on the PlayStation. You spend all day playing while other ethnic groups are creating the PlayStations that suck you into this mindless garbage. You are not focusing on your grades and so you are doing the crime of PlayStation, hooking school, doing blunts. You are doing the crime of not going to class, and not paying attention, not doing your homework, but you are not ready for the punishment that comes with that. You are not ready for the punishment of Ridlin, and the punishment of special education. You are not ready for the punishment of being stereotyped and written off. You are not ready for the punishment of teachers thinking you can not make it and you are not about anything, so I am not going to spend time with you.

We are doing crimes but we are not considering the time. We are doing sexual crimes of so-called "safe sex" with condoms, but we're not ready for the punishment when we find out that the condom breaks or the condom does not work. Then we have the punishment of HIV. We find that there is no cure and we are not ready and prepared to deal with the punishment. It is too great. Sexual crimes run rampant. We're watching all kinds of things on TV. We're not guarding what our young people see. We are not talking to our young people about sex and we are committing a crime. So when our teenager shows up pregnant, we are not ready for the punishment for us being silent parents. All kinds of crime, and we are not considering, young people, what happens as a result of the crime.

In the story of Cain and Abel, Cain says to his brother, Abel, "Let's go out into the field." While they were in the field, Cain attacked his brother, Abel, and killed him. You know what I find, young people? When you go and do the crime and the punishment comes, just like Cain you get mad at the wrong person. Cain got mad at Abel, but it was the Lord who rebuked Cain's sacrifice; misplaced anger is what I call it. The Lord said, "Cain, if you give me the right sacrifice, won't I honor it? Won't I hold you in high esteem?" Instead of Cain doing a mental reflection, the self- introspection and the psychological evaluation; instead of Cain really sitting down, shutting up, taking a moment to stop, look and listen; instead of him asking, "What do I need to do differently?" Cain bypassed himself and misplaced his anger. He dealt with his brother and he did it in such a way, as if he was just so smooth, like we do sometimes. Not you all, I mean like when other people get ready to stab somebody in the back. They find a nice soft spot. "Come on. Let's go out to dinner together. Let's go out to a movie, so I can find a nice soft spot to stab you in the back." Cain misplaced his anger. Don't we see that a lot, young people? You leave out of a house where you do not pay the mortgage, or an apartment on which you do not pay the rent, wearing clothes that you do not buy, after having slept in a bed that you have not bought, smoothed out the wrinkles in your clothes on an ironing board that you do not put up or take down and when your parents require you to make up your bed and take care of your room, you get mad at the very one who provided you with what you have. The punishment does not fit the crime.

You know when you are struggling and the teacher says that you are getting a C because you are not doing your work? You go home and tell your parents that your teacher talked down to you. Never doing the mental reflection, never looking at yourself and trying to see what it is that you need to do to make yourself better; just like Cain, you are killing the wrong people. We ought to be killing the ignorance in our heads. We ought to be killing what we see on TV. We ought to be killing the soap operas. We ought to be killing all the stuff we see out here in the street. Do not kill Abel. Abel did not do anything. All Abel did was give unto the Lord that which was the Lord's. Be reminded, young people, for the crimes that you do the punishment can be much greater than you think. Don't do the crime of talking back to your mama or daddy, if you are not prepared to receive the punishment of a backhand. Don't do the crime of getting D's and C's and then when your parents take away from you those things that you like, you get mad and do not speak to them for a week, or two weeks, or three weeks. They took your game that you did not pay for, stopped you from watching a TV that you didn't buy but you get mad at them when you're the one bringing home D's? I know people who go to private schools. Their parents pay $10-$12,000 a year for their kids to come home with F's and D's. I would break my child's neck! The time will come, young people, when you might not have everything the Lord has blessed your parents to get. And you are not ready for the punishment of catching the bus like I had to do in 20- degree weather. You are not ready for that!

Then the Lord said to Cain, "Where is your brother?" The Lord asked Cain a question. Now, that's kind of silly. I do not want to insult you. Why does the Lord need to ask a question when He knows everything? Why does He need to ask Cain where's Abel when He was right there when Cain was killing Abel? That does not make sense. Does it? This is what I found out. The Lord showed me that He was really giving Cain an opportunity to tell the truth. Sometimes your parents, or your teachers, or your pastor, or your friends know you have messed up. They know you have made a mistake. They have been where you are before and all they want you to do is to tell the truth. Instead of telling the truth, you say, "I don't know." Why didn't you come straight home from school? "Uh, I had band practice." You have never even joined a band.

Just like our parents have done with us, the Lord was giving Cain an opportunity to redeem himself, to open up and admit what God already knew. It is just like when God called to Adam and said, "Adam, where are you?" God knew where Adam was. Don't do the crime if you can't do the time. Cain goes on. You could tell he was still angry with the Lord. Cain messed around and told the Lord, "I don't know. Am I my brother's keeper?" Still mad at the Lord, he had committed murder and he was still mad at the Lord. The Bible says, do not let the Lord's sun go down on your anger. Sometimes people think that getting back at other people will make them feel better. It is not going to make you feel better. Cain was still upset, still mad at the Lord.

Cain was still upset. Cain was still angry. "Lord, am I my brother's keeper? He was my brother, but you created him." Cain was too stubborn to go and apologize to the Lord. Young folks, Cain was probably 15, 16, or 17, around your age. He knew everything. Even though he had not lived as long as his parents, he knew everything. He knew everything, so he kept trying to tell everybody what he knew instead of listening to what his parents said. "Boy, I have been where you're going. You have not been where I have been." Young folks, you had better listen to what I am saying. Do not get so grown, bull headed, stubborn, and proud that you think that you are too big to apologize.

Parents, it is a good chance that Adam and Eve did not share the probable consequences of a possible crime against God. Maybe they were too proud. Maybe they were trying to be so holy and righteous that they did not want the young folks to know what they did at their age when they were teens. We have to share what happened in our lives when we did the crimes that we were not ready for. We've got to let our young people know. "Listen, I was where you are. Yeah, I might have smoked some weed. Yeah, I might have had sex before I was married. You know you did not come before we got married. But, let me talk about the mistakes I made so you do not have to do the same crime, so you do not have to do the same time and the same punishment."

Maybe Adam and Eve did not say anything to Cain and Abel. Sometimes I find parents are so deep into the Lord now; so saved now. They are so deep that they do not wear their skirts above their knees now. Because they are so deep now they forgot when they were 17 and had that figure eight, how they were flaunting all up and down the avenue.

Another theory is this. Maybe Adam and Eve did tell Cain and Abel the rules of God and maybe they chose to ignore their parents. Young folks, how many times have we ignored our parents? How many times have you lied to your parents, knowing that your parents knew the truth? You still never came back and told the truth. Let me tell you a story. My daughter got into a bad habit a couple of weeks ago of lying for no reason at all, just telling stories, no reason to lie. Her mother would ask her something simple. She would tell a lie. I am praying for this child because I know her mother's patience will run out. Well, she told one lie one night and my wife lost all her patience and beat the devil out of her. That is where the saying comes from, "beat the devil out of her." The punishment was so severe; the crying was so loud that my four-year-old son came into the room after the beating and said, "Mama, I'm sorry for losing my bracelet". He wanted to make sure that he was in the clear. "Tell the truth and shame the devil." That is what the elders used to say. Look at Verse 10. The Lord said, "What have you done? Listen," that's what the Lord said, "Listen, listen the blood of your brother is crying out from the ground" because you did a crime that you were not ready for. My young brothers and sisters, the blood of your ancestors is crying from the ground. Every time you do not go to school the blood is crying out, every time you do not read the Word of God. Their eyes were poked out just because they wanted to learn how to read, hands were cut off, just for opening up a book. Every time you ignore education and every time you do not do your best, the blood, the blood, the blood of your ancestors starts crying out. All of the hundreds of years of lynching are crying out. It is crying out, crying out. Every time you disrespect your parents, the blood of your ancestors from Africa, those children who were snatched from their villages are crying out.

Listen! The Lord says when you do crimes and you do not consider what is going on, when you do these sinful crimes, the blood of the people you affect cries out. You know what I find adults? This is our fault. We have not taught our children their history, because if they knew their history they would appreciate what they have got a little more. They would learn a little harder. You see, the Asians teach their children their history. The Jews teach their children their history. The Caucasians, we are forced to learn their history, but we do not teach our children our history. I have my children sit down with me. We do not just watch Roots, we watch Amistad and we watch everything that talks about the struggle. We watch everything that talks about the Middle Passage. My child needs to know how many people died so that she can go to school and hold her head up. I want her to get on the Internet and read so I tell her the blood of her ancestors is crying out. When you show laziness, the blood, the blood, the blood, just like Abel's blood, the blood of your ancestors cries out.

Let me tell you this, young folks, because some of you may not be familiar. Our ancestors would steal away. That means they would leave their little huts that they were in, their little shacks, go down to the water and just open up the Bible or just open up a book. They did not understand. They were illiterate. That is because it was against the law for them to read but they would risk it anyway. They were trying to read, trying to figure out, was there any salvation in the word of God? You ought not to take for granted that you can read and not have your eyes plucked out. You ought not to take for granted that somebody actually wants to teach you how to go forward.

The blood; your brother's blood cries out from the ground and now here comes the punishment. Now you are under a curse. The ground that God created when He said all the vegetation, come forth, and it was good? The ground that the Lord separated from the water in the beginning? This same ground that God cursed because of Adam and Eve's sin? Now the ground opened up and received the blood of Abel, at the hand of Cain. When you work the ground the Lord said, no longer is the ground going to be friendly to you. So now all of the stuff that you eat, even all of the vegetables, will have pesticides in them. You do not know what you are eating because you have got pesticides to preserve them because the ground is no longer friendly. That is why some farmers are raising chickens and pumping steroids in them. That is why at ten years of age you have got the body of a 20-year-old. You're sucking down all those drugs because the ground is no longer yielding its produce to you. The red meat, the mad cow disease, all this stuff that you suck into your body no wonder you do not understand why you are crazy. All that sugar that you get full of chemicals? You love that sugar. And you do not know why you are addicted to sugar. Why are so many of our children on Ridlin? Why do so many young boys get kicked out of school or put into special education. You can not focus because of your diet.

The greatest punishment you can ever have, in terms of committing a crime against the Lord, Jesus Christ, is to have God turn His back to you. You will feel as if you are alone and all by yourself. But, I tell young people

God is omniscient. God is everywhere. So it is no need in you coming home when your parents are at work thinking that nobody knows what you are doing. The Lord is there. Your parents tell you to get off the phone. It is no need in you waiting until they turn the light off to pick the phone back up; the Lord is there. You can't hide from the Lord. I hear the Lord saying to you now, where are you? What are you doing? Shouldn't you be in the bed? The Lord is there. Cain says it this way, "Listen Lord. Now you know I make my living by the ground. I am a farmer. I can not live. I can't sustain myself and what you are telling me about my very survival is more than I can handle. I know I did the crime."

Here is a guy who offered the wrong sacrifice to the Lord, killed one of the Lord's people and got the nerve to mention to the Lord, out of his mouth, that the Lord's punishment is too great. Young people, now that is bold! That is like when your mama goes and buys you $140 pair of Scottie Pippin's and you say you want a $180 pair of Jordan's. That is bold! Your mama and daddy tell you to vacuum the room that you stay in and you say you are tired of cleaning up. That is bold! It's bold when you take a jacket out of the house that you did not buy and leave it somewhere or let somebody else wear it and not bring it home. That is bold!

Some of you all would not be alive today if it were not for the hand of God. But it is bold. Cain is telling the Lord that his punishment is more than he can bear. I told you this. I said sometimes when you plan to do a crime you think that this might happen. This punishment might happen, but what you do not know is that the Lord might have something different in store for you. Now, this is to adults, too. This is not just for young folks. You go out there and step out. You think you are going to get you a little piece of side action. You say, well the worse thing that can happen is that I get caught. I might have to spend a few days on the couch. But you did not take into consideration that you could be getting divorced. You might be out of the house and paying child support. Bold! The punishment is too great. I can see Cain now. Now this is the part that is called the judgment. He has done the crime. He is already at the courthouse. Now he is in the wake of judgment so he is throwing himself on the mercy of the Lord. Lord, I know I did it, but it is too much for me to bear. He says, "today you are driving me from the land and I will be hidden from your presence. I will be a restless wanderer upon the earth." But the real reason he was scared was because he said that whoever finds me would kill me. You see, it was the threat of death that really made Cain scared. Young people, death is all around you. Sin is lurking at your door. I am not trying to tell you to be all high and mighty and try to be something that you are not. You will make mistakes in your life. Just understand death is all around you. I am not talking about physical death. If I can kill you mentally, you are already dead. I do not have any problems with you. If I can make you think that you are more American than you are African, I do not ever have to worry about you trying to liberate your people. If I can make you think that a C is all right and the Asians know that an A+ is better, then I have already killed you.

Cain died mentally and spiritually when he killed his brother. When you misplace our anger, you find yourself in the Lord's courtroom. You find the angels up here. You find the sons and daughters of God over here. You find yourself in the heavenly courtroom. And we have all been there, young people. Nobody is exempt. We all have sinned and we have all done crimes. If it were not for the hand of the Lord snatching us, we would not be here today. We are not standing here all grand and prissy. What we are telling you is that sometimes you do the crime and sometimes you can not handle the time, but there is good news!

Verse 15 says that even though you have given me the wrong sacrifice and even though Cain, you did not give me your tithes, you came to church and did not give me your first. Even though you murdered your brother…I do not know about you, but I have murdered some people in my life. I murdered some friends by talking about them. Sometimes I have gossiped on them. Sometimes I did not help them out and I murdered them. The Lord knows. You are guilty and the Lord knows who you are. Look what happened in the holy courtroom. In Verse 15, the Lord says, do not even worry about somebody killing you. This is not going to happen. He sends out a summons on the world. If anyone tries to kill Cain, vengeance will be mine seven times. Then he puts a mark on Cain, letting people know, do not touch Cain. I know you heard about his reputation. I know you heard he used to be a drug addict and a crack addict. I know you heard he used to be in special education. I know you heard that Cain was a murderer and that all he did was hang out on the street and disrespect his parents. And he was a teen father. Forget about all of that. I am going to put a mark on him and a mark on you because you're my child. You know what that says to me? God's mercy endures forever. All I am saying to you, young people, is that there are some people who will try to condemn you. There are some people who will say, "Give them the chair". Some people will say, "Kick him out of school," but the Lord will say, "Not so, because I've got a mark on this boy. I've got a mark on this girl. And wheresoever they walk, goodness and mercy is going to follow them all the way because I am the Lord and I will show mercy on whomever I want to show mercy." Here's a personal testimony; I did a lot of crime in my day. If it were not for me crying out, "Lord, I can not handle the punishment...."

I heard the prosecutor say, "He has got to go. He did the crime...guilty on 15 counts of murder, guilty on 15 counts of hooking school, guilty on 15 counts of not going to church, not reading the Word, ignoring his history. Guilty! Guilty! Guilty! Then, I heard the Big Judge up top saying, "I know the evidence is stacked against him, but case dismissed! I have got a mark on this child. He's going to do great things." All I am saying, young people, is you might have gotten away with some stuff in your life but it is not because you have been so good. God has placed this mark of anointing on you. There is a purpose for your life. God has called you. Cain went on to have children. The fifth generation child became the harp and flute player;

the sixth generation became the ones to develop tools. All I am saying is there's a purpose for your life. Sometimes you find yourself saying, "Lord, the punishment is too great for me to bear!" But I know somebody who paid the price for your sins, somebody who paid the price for your crimes. He went to Calvary for your crimes. Even though you messed up, do not put yourself down. All you got to do is read John 3:16 and say, "for God so loved the world." Even before you did the crime, He knew what you were going to do. That is why He sent His son so that if you confess with your mouth and believe in your heart that He will wipe away your sins, you shall be saved. You shall receive power. You shall receive power. That is what the Lord did for you.

So I sympathize with Cain because sometimes the punishment is too great. That is why I praise the Lord because His mercy endures forever. Every time I get home, I think about all the money I have blown and the Lord still puts food on my table because His mercy endures forever. Every time I go to bed mad at my child, the Lord wakes me up and gives me another chance with him. I know that the Lord's mercy endures forever. Every time I walk the streets at night, I am not scared of anybody because His mercy endures forever. I did not wait until I was married to have sex, but every time I think about how the Lord snatched me out before I stayed too long; that has nothing to do with me, His mercy endures forever. Even though people are hating on me, His mercy endures forever. Young people, the teachers do not like you. That does not matter. There is a mark of mercy on your forehead. People trying to get you into gangs. That does not matter, because His mercy endures forever. Lesbians are trying to get you. That does not matter. Homosexuals are trying to get you, that does not matter. Blunt smokers trying to get you, that does not matter. Folks hooking school trying to get you, that does not matter. Special is education trying to get you. That does not matter because the Lord's got a mark on your life and His mercy endures forever. Do not let the blood of your ancestors have been shed in vain.

Don't Do the Crime. Review Questions

1. Who was the oldest between Cain and Abel?
2. What are some of the crimes young people are committing against their bodies?
3. What are some of the punishments of these crimes?
4. What are some educational crimes we are committing?
5. What are some of the punishments of these crimes?
6. Where and why did Cain attack his brother, Abel?
7. What was Cain's response to God's question about Abel's whereabouts?
8. What did God say was crying out from the ground that let God know that Abel was dead?
9. What did Cain say about the punishment that God gave him for his crime?
10. What did God do to Cain to protect him from being killed?

Here is the gospel story of Jesus when he was around 12 years old and
making his first traditional pilgrimage to celebrate the Passover Feast.
Passover was an annual celebration of the Exodus event. It was one of
three feasts where males age 12 and older were required to be present.
The other two feasts were the Feast of Weeks and Feasts of Tabernacles.

Power in Breaking Tradition
Luke 2:41-52

Every Sunday since the Day of Pentecost as recorded in Acts, Chapter 2, those of us who follow the teachings of Jesus Christ, come together to have church. For many of us every Monday, Tuesday, or Wednesday we come to choir rehearsal, Bible study or mid-week services. Many of us come because these are and have become established traditions in the life of the body of Christ. Many of us are continuing to live by rituals and traditions. Sadly, many of us never seriously questioned the origin of these church traditions. We never questioned why there were never any women preachers. We just know that the tradition was handed down and that must have been the way that God intended it to be. Even here in our biblical story, we observe the Holy family practicing their religious tradition going to Jerusalem to celebrate Passover. After the Passover Festival, they started to return home, as was the custom, or tradition. They were not traveling by themselves. There was a caravan. This means a whole lot of folk traveled together to Jerusalem and there were a whole lot of folk that came back together. The text says that the festival ended. The boy, Jesus, stayed behind in Jerusalem, but his parents did not know it. His parents did not know where their son was.

Assuming that he was in the group of travelers, they went a day's journey. Now as a parent of three, I can identify with Joseph and Mary. I, too, have experienced walking somewhere and feeling confident that my children were right behind me only to turn around and find them way back taking their own precious time in their own world. The story goes on to tell us that they started to look for Jesus among their relatives and friends. When they did not find him they returned to Jerusalem to search for him. After three days, they found Jesus in the temple sitting among the teachers listening to them and asking them questions. All who heard Jesus were amazed at his answers and when his parents saw him they were astonished. That is putting it mildly. Mary was a dark-skinned Jewish woman, as were all Jews in the first century and prior to the destruction of the Temple of Jerusalem in AD 70. I can imagine this Madonna had her hands on her hips with her neck rolling and her hands in the grab-and-choke position. She said, "Boy, have you lost your eternal earthly mind? What in the hell is wrong with you? Why have you gone crazy and had us looking for you for three days? When I get you back to Nazareth, I am going to beat you like you stole something!" (Rev. Rudy's divine emphasis). Jesus said to them, just like our modern day young folk, "Whatcha looking for me for? I thought I told you I was doing my own thing. You did know I must be about my Father's business, in my Father's house?" But they did not understand what he said to them because (if I can add my interpretation here) he spoke with an unknown post-millennium tongue. Then he went down with them, came back home and was obedient to them. You know when he returned back home what Mary did to him? The Bible is clear. After they had gotten home, then he was obedient. Let me break it down to you. Sometimes your parents will say to you before a beating, "You did not listen to me this time, but after this beating you will listen the next time."

The tradition was that they went to offer sacrifice and they went to worship. I am going to show you the parallels. This story is so similar to what we do today, parents. Our children come with us to church, but in the midst of our being stuck into doing things just as we have always done them, our children are in our midst but just like young Jesus, they are lost. They are lost in the church while we are singing in the choir. They are not listening to the message. They are lost. Just like Joseph and Mary, we assume that our children are growing up in a Christian manner just because they went with us to church. They go with us to church on Sunday. We drag them to Sunday school. We drag them to Bible study. We assume that they are growing in Christ, when they are really lost. And they do not know how to tell you that they are not getting anything out of the service or the sermon.

Some of us have become so traditional that we are no longer spiritual. You see our grandparents and our elders were and are spiritual. They did not need the preacher to tell them when to pray. They felt something in their spirit. They would say, "I need to get down on my knees because my child is in trouble." Grandmother and grandfather would go out on the porch and smell the rain. That was spiritual. When you arrive at the point where you can come in God's house and not speak to your neighbor, church service is traditional, not spiritual. But when you are spiritual and you come into God's house, you are happy to be around other Christians. You are happy to be around the body of Christ and you want to speak to everybody you come in contact with and then you know that you are spiritual. Traditional people pay their tithes just because they are scared of going to hell. Spiritual people understand that the more they give, the more they receive. Spiritual people tithe because they know that the Lord will open up the window of heaven and pour out a blessing that there will not be room enough to receive.

Allow me to talk about Joseph and Mary. I do not care if you call me the Anti-Christ. They need to be talked about because they seemed more traditional than they were spiritual. They were so caught up in going to Jerusalem to sacrifice and doing their traditional service that they did not even feel that their child was not with them.

There used to be a time when our parents did not have to put their children on leashes like other ethnic groups. First of all they scared the hell out of you. "You move more than one second away from me, I'll kill you." Other races put their children on leashes like animals. We did not have to do that. Mama had a look and you knew that if you were in that mall acting a fool, that look came. Joseph and Mary were so traditional that they went 24 hours and did not know that their own child was not with them. Does that not sound like us? So pressed to get to that church on time, we forgot to even speak to our children in a positive manner. So pressed to get to choir rehearsal, we do not even ask our children, "How was your day?" We do not ask them what they dealt with in school. We do not ask them, "What kind of demons haunted you today?" We are so pressed to get them in God's house because Bible study starts at 7:00 that our children are suffering and we do not even know it. So traditional that they lost the Savior; they lost the Lord and Savior. Do not talk about Joseph and Mary. Sometimes we are so caught up about coming to church that we leave church and have never come in contact with the Savior. You have been to a two-hour choir rehearsal and the Lord never moved in your soul. You went to a two-hour usher board meeting and you never felt the presence of God move in the building. Do not look down on Joseph and Mary because some of us are just like them so caught up in keeping "tradition". We are so busy keeping up the tradition that our children, even though they are in church, are only one step away from walking out of the door. They are one blunt away from getting locked up or getting killed. Your daughter is one offer away of that young boy who will get her pregnant or give her the AIDS virus. And we are in church. We are saved. We are sanctified, fire baptized. We come to church. We are running for the Lord, but our children are dying in the pews. If you want to get some power in your parenting, if you want to get some power in your church, if you want to bring the youth from the suburbs and the ghettos, you have to break some traditions.

The Pharisees and the Scribes talked about Jesus because he broke some traditions. Tradition says that you should not heal on the Sabbath. Jesus says to forget your rules. This man needs to be healed. I do not care what day it is. Some of our young folk need God on Wednesday. They cannot wait for Sunday. They need to be in God's house on Monday. They cannot wait for Thursday's Bible study. The people need to be healed. These young people need to be ministered to. You cannot get stuck in traditions. Two services on Sunday, three points from the preacher, altar prayer, mid-week service and you send them out to the wolves. We have no power in the church because we are so stuck in tradition. I found out that some elders do not want to let go of certain traditions because we have been taught a certain way. There are certain traditions we need to hold on to. When I was growing up, if you did not go to church, you did not do anything on Sunday. If you did not go to church, you did not eat. If you did not go to church, you did not watch TV. You did not go outside. Those are good traditions. There are other traditions we have to shed. If a young girl's wardrobe is pants right now, do not make her feel badly about coming into God's house. Break that tradition! You let her come into God's house and watch God change her wardrobe. Stop trying to do God's job. So, Jesus broke tradition. When they came back and found him, they asked him what was he doing? Had he lost his mind? He asked them did they not understand his purpose in life? Our children have been given a gift and a purpose from God and because we do not understand it, we shoot it down. The vision God has given some of these young folk, you cannot understand it. You cannot comprehend it, but please do not shoot it down. These young folk see dancers everywhere. They see misguided rap stars. They see hood rats and they are dancing. They are shaking their thing. They are singing about all manner of evil and wickedness. Then they come in church and want to sing. They want to sing righteously. They want to develop a praise dance team. And there is something about your tradition that says we do not do that in this church. It does not take all of that. But the minute you see an adolescent and she is completely naked then you say, "Oh, it does not make any sense child." You are correct. It does not make any sense because you should have broken tradition and let her develop a dance team right in the house of God in the name of God. We are now blaming the children. How are you going to blame a ten-year-old who knows every hip-hop dance? It is your fault. Our children watch too much TV. Whose fault is that? Who bought the TV? Who pays the electric bill? Who is the parent? My children know not to turn that TV on in the morning. Do not turn that TV on as soon as you come home. Read a book. The TV is addictive. This generation has been given something so special, but they are so scared to bring it to you because it is different. So that even in God's house they are not free to be who they want to be. How do people in the world have more freedom than the people who are free in Christ? You sing the song, "I am free. Praise the Lord. I am free, no more chains holding me." Then, why are our children still shackled up with tradition? Break the shackles. Loose the fetters. Understand what God has given these young folk. We have some beautiful young folk. Number one, they are in the Lord. Number two, they are in God's house. If they are in God's house, that is where we want them to stay. I ask, "Do they have a basketball team?" If not, start one. I ask, "Do they have a Holy Ghost step team?" If not, start one. I ask them, do they have a praise dance ministry? If not, start one. I ask, "What in the hell do you do in God's house?" Young folk answer, "We come to sing." There has to be more to Christ than that my brothers and sisters. Jesus did not walk around preaching in a P. Diddy, Tommy Hilfiger, nor a tailored made suit with processed hair, gold on all his fingers, holding altar call in a traditional manner. Jesus just did it. When somebody needed to be healed, he healed him or her. When he was hungry, he just ate. When the Lord told Him it was time to fast, he fasted. He was not all stuck. Although, he was traditional, he was not a rigid fundamentalist.

We follow everybody else more than we follow Christ. There is more judging going on in the church towards our young folk, than anywhere else. When I checked the Bible, the Bible said that the Son of Man did not come to judge but to save (John 3:17). So if that is the Word of the Lord, then why is it when somebody comes in who looks a little different than our traditional look, we turn our nose up and we cast judgment? There are things that the Lord did not say that we are doing and we will take it to our grave that it is right. Jesus never said it; but we said it was right because it is the way we have been told. We do not know who said it. We do not know who told us, but we know it must be the Gospel. You cannot find it in the book, but it must be the Gospel. You cannot see where Jesus said it, even if you get a Bible with the red print. You cannot find where Jesus said it, but it must be the Gospel because that is "what I grew up on." You do not take into account that the preacher could have been crazy. You do not take into account that the preacher could have been drunk. You do not take into account that the preacher could have had a slave mentality. All you know is that this is the way you came up. The preacher said it, and that is the way it is. If you do not have your own relationship with God and study the text, then the preacher does you no good. When you go before God, you cannot blame the preacher because you did not study the Word.

Finally, and here is the good news in this text. When they searched for Jesus for three days; they went to their friends and relatives but they did not find him. After three days they went to God's house and there they found your Savior in God's house sitting at the feet of elders asking questions.

The great thing about your young folk who are in the church is the fact that you do not have to go to the ghettos of America to find them; they are not home watching TV. They are not outside smoking blunts. The good news is that when you came into God's house, you found them in the choir. When you came in God's house, you found them in the sanctuary. And that is the good news. You have some good young folk. They are in God's house. And if you open up your eyes, if you understand the power in breaking tradition;

then you will recognize that if they are in God's house, then God can work in their life. God is subject to have His way. As long as these young folk are in the presence of the people, God can move on their behalf. This means adults you have to be glad that they are in the house of God because in God's house there is joy. In God's house there is peace. In God's house, there is understanding. There is a lot of encouragement in God's house. There is a lot of wisdom in these elders in God's house. So, rejoice beloved in the Lord because your young folk are in God's house. You do what you have to do to keep them in God's house. Do not lose them to BET (Buffoon Entertainment Television)! Do not lose them to the sports team! Do not lose them to the mall! You do what you need to do to keep them in God's house. Throw a block party if you have to, a go-go if you have to, you just keep them in God's house. If you keep them in God's house, God will change their lives. If you keep them in God's house, God will change their wardrobe. If you keep them in God's house, they will not get pregnant, they will not catch AIDS, they will not start smoking, they will not get locked up, they will not get shot down if you keep them in God's house.

Power in Breaking Tradition. Review Questions

1. How old was Jesus when he made his first pilgrimage to Jerusalem to celebrate the Passover Feast?
2. After the Passover Feast was completed, what did Jesus do while his parents headed back home?
3. How many days passed before Joseph and Mary found Jesus?
4. Where did they find Jesus?
5. The author says that many parents have become more _____ as opposed to_____.

6. What are some examples of the above two answers?
7. Make a list of some of your church traditions that bore young folk to death.
8. What exciting new millennial activities is your church sponsoring for this generation of young people?
9. Does your church have a youth pastor, a youth sports team, bowling league etc? If not, have you asked for any of the above to be started?
10. Should church be the place so attractive to God's people that we would long to be in the church all the time like our Hebrew ancestors? See Psalm 84, for example.

Epilogue
The Shepherd's Voice

The dilemma facing our youth today should be a major concern to all of us. The "hope factor" in our communities has been absorbed by the deteriorating social, economic, political and spiritual state in which we find ourselves. The problems our youth face are endemic, epidemic and pandemic. They are endemic because they have become a part of the very fabric of our society, epidemic because they have gotten out of hand and pandemic because they are everywhere.

HIV-AIDS is running rampant and threatening to annihilate an entire generation. Street violence and crime have reached monumental proportions. Teen pregnancy is steadily rising and there is a growing "disconnect" between youth and their parents.

Uncertainty, insecurity, disillusionment, confusion, frustration and fear have gripped entire communities causing many to ask: "Is there a future? What will the future be like? How can we secure and solidify the future of our youth?"

But the conditions facing our youth did not happen overnight, and ignoring them or leaving them for "others" to solve will not suddenly cause the scenario to change for the better.

Rev. Rudolph Stewart III addresses these very serious questions and the vital issue of preserving our youth in the midst of these turbulent times.

Not only does Rev. Stewart raise the relevant question to the youth often stated by parents, "What the Hell is wrong with you?" but he also offers a prophetic guide to both parents and youth alike to cure the problems they each face.

Our communities are pregnant with a future generation and neglect of that generation is abuse of the future. If the future is to be better than the present, the youth must be the agency through which things will be made better.

In this very bold, powerful presentation Rev. Rudy lets parents and youth alike understand that the power to create better communication between parents and youth is with them in the present. The author offers cogent, incisive approaches and remedies to the very deep and profound dilemmas facing parents and youth. In this volume, Rev. Rudy demands, at all costs, that parents seek to understand, protect and preserve the youth not only because they are the heritage of Almighty God, but also because they are also the future of the present.

Our communities are pregnant with a generation and we all know that the condition of the mother affects the health of the child. Physically, whatever the mother eats, drinks or inhales will be transferred to the offspring. Psychologically and spiritually, we know that this reality is also true – the thoughts, feelings, values and perspectives of both parents (father and mother) also have an impact on the mental and spiritual health of the child. Rev. Rudy offers viable solutions to insure that parents will not be guilty of generational abortion.

I highly recommend this book to both parents and youth who have the common desire to fulfill God's purpose in producing a dynamic, divinely prepared next generation.

Rev. Willie F. Wilson
Senior Pastor, Union Temple Baptist Church
Author, Releasing The Power Within: The Genius of Jesus Revealed

About the Author

Rev. Rudolph Stewart III is married to Jerlys Stewart. Together they have three children, Imani Diane, Rudolph IV and Jeriah Diane. Rev. Rudy has a Bachelor of Arts degree in Radio, TV and Film from Howard University School of Communications. He also holds a Masters of Divinity degree from Howard University School of Divinity where he graduated summa cum laude with a 4.0 GPA, earning him the Dean's Award and the Vernon Johns Preaching Award.

Rev. Rudy is co-professor of the *Survey of the New Testament* at Howard University and professor of *Biblical Examples of Male/Female Relationships* at Union Temple Baptist Church. He has developed, implemented and directed an African-centered school called Nation Building Time (NBT) with specific focus on reinforcing standard curriculum and melding African cultural concepts that are not typically taught in school. NBT offers a broad range of cultural and academic subjects including African drumming and dance, hand and line dancing, praise dancing, natural hair care, Swahili, Twi, Spanish and story time. For the last three years Rev. Rudy has served as a teaching assistant to Dr. Cain Hope Felder, Chairman of the Masters of Divinity program at Howard University School of Divinity. Rev. Rudy was also youth pastor at the First Baptist Church on Minnesota Avenue.

Prior to going into a full-time preaching/teaching ministry, Rev. Rudy served as vice chairman of the Interagency Consortium on Adolescent Pregnancy for the City of Alexandria, VA, a conglomerate of 30+ agencies in Alexandria aimed at the reduction of adolescent pregnancy. He also designed and implemented the Akoben Male Mentoring Program, an African-centered, city-wide mentoring program with a focus on rescuing young African-American males labeled "at-risk". Rev. Rudy was also the director of the Male Teen Responsibility Project for the Northern Virginia Urban League. The emphasis of the project was to teach African-American and Latino adolescent males the social, psychological, academic and physical skills necessary for successfully navigating through their pubescent years.

From 1992-2000, Rev. Rudy designed and operated the first African-centered group home for youth ages 12-19 in Washington, DC called the "House of Seven Steps". Rev. Rudy created the concept of this group home based on the seven principles of the Nguzo Saba. These principles are Umoja, Kujichagulia, Ujima, Ujamaa, Nia, Kuumba, and Imani. These seven principles, the foundation of Kwanzaa, a celebration of African heritage and liberation, also served as the foundation for correcting years of sexual, social and mental abuse perpetrated against these young men. God has shown Rev. Rudy that the key to healing and restoration of these young men was in an accurate presentation and identification of their African culture, history and religion. It was during the 10-year operation of the group home that he realized his divine prophetic gift to minister to the broken relationships between youths and parents.

Rev. Rudy's call to biblical scholarship forced him to suspend his ministry of healing through comedy and focus on perfection in biblical scholarship. Prior to that, he hosted several television and radio shows including a national TV show on The Renaissance Network called "Culture Shock", a political television show on the America's Voice Network called "Off the Fence" and a live radio program via AOL live chat. In addition, Rev. Rudy hosted and engineered "Rev. Rudy's Gospel Spot" a venue in which the people of God came out and enjoyed wholesome comedy, inspiration through poetry, jazz and gospel singing.

As a writer/producer, Rev. Rudy created and performed in a radio program with gospel station WYCB, 1340 AM in the Greater Washington Area entitled "Lessons Taught, Lessons Learned" which he adapted into a biblical/church comedy play currently being sold on video.

As a gospel comedian, Rev. Rudy performed in various media including, but not limited to BET Teen Summit, Warner Theater of Washington, DC, touring the musical theater production entitled "Sneaky" at historic Lincoln Theater and the Progressive Baptist National Convention '99 in Washington, DC.

Although Rev. Rudy is not currently ministering in spiritual humor, he uses this divine gift in his writing, sermon delivery and counseling. Most recently, Dr. Cain Hope Felder invited him to present a biblical exegesis of Psalm 46 at a study tour of Egypt and the Holy Land. Rev. Rudy has done missionary work in orphanages and hospices in Port Au Prince, Haiti.

Rev. Rudy is committed to regenerating and restoring the African American family with particular interest on husband/wife relationships and parenting. His overall focus is to keep alive the connection and value of his African homeland and renew the pride of African culture here in America.